EXPERIENCING SPIRITUAL REVIVAL

Renewing Your Desire for God

MARGARET FEINBERG
FOREWORD BY LISA HARPER

THOMAS NELSON
Since 1798

NASHVILLE   DALLAS   MEXICO CITY   RIO DE JANEIRO

Published in Nashville, Tennessee, by Thomas Nelson. Thomas Nelson is a trademark of Thomas Nelson, Inc.

Thomas Nelson, Inc., titles may be purchased in bulk for educational, business, fund-raising, or sales promotional use. For information, please email SpecialMarkets@ ThomasNelson.com.

All Scripture quotations are taken from the the New King James Version. © 1982 by Thomas Nelson, Inc. Used by permission. All rights reserved.

Scripture quotations marked NIV are taken from The Holy Bible, *New International Version*®, *NIV*®. Copyright © 1973, 1978, 1984, 2011 by Biblica, Inc.™ Used by permission of Zondervan. All rights reserved worldwide. www.zondervan.com

Page design: Crosslin Creative

978-1-4016-7913-2

Printed in China

HB 09.30.2022

Contents

Foreword

After twenty-five years of constant air travel, I've become a frustrated frequent flyer. I don't like squeezing shampoo and conditioner into wee bottles to keep from having my carry-on bag confiscated. I don't like taking off my shoes in the security line. I don't like holding my arms over my head, sucking in my stomach, and getting zapped in the "naked machine." And I really don't like wedging into seats configured for a supermodel's rear end only to have some self-absorbed businessman plop down next to me and hog the armrest. Needless to say, I don't always *enjoy* the commuting experience.

But not too long ago, God restored some of my going-from-one-place-to-another gladness. I was en route from Atlanta to Chicago and was hunkered down in my typical flight-endurance posture—reading *People* magazine with iPod earbuds in and avoiding eye contact with other passengers—when I noticed a commotion making its way through first class. A little boy about four or five years old was galloping down the aisle, all but dragging an exhausted-looking woman. I thought to myself, *I betcha a million bucks their seats are next to mine.* And sure enough, the Energizer Bunny boy bounced into my row, followed by his all-but-comatose mama. I managed a faint smile at them and secretly hoped she'd laced his juice box with Dramamine.

No such luck.

It soon became obvious that he was not only having his first flying experience but had inhaled a heavy dose of sugar beforehand. He wiggled wildly in the window seat and peered out the porthole, loudly declaring his observations. His words increased in speed and volume during taxi and takeoff until his voice was a shriek audible only to dogs and exasperated seatmates. But the screeching stopped abruptly once we were in the air.

I thought, *Oh no, he's probably swallowed a peanut.* Glancing over to make sure he was okay, I was graced by the sight of a child completely entranced. His eyes were wide and his chubby fists were clasped to his chest. When he recovered his voice and resumed his commentary, I closed my book, leaned back, and smiled as he compared the clouds to cotton candy. That precious, noisy towhead reminded me not to let minor inconveniences steal a major chunk of my joy.

Because our earth isn't Eden, we have to be intentional about shrugging off little annoyances like humidity, bad hair days, and Spanx, and focus instead on the wonderful gifts God has given us to enjoy—things like the myriad of beautiful colored leaves in the fall, the amazing smell of hot coffee on a cold morning, and the mercies of God we receive new *every single morning* (Lam. 3:22–23). Our hope is that this Bible study guide on *Experiencing Spiritual Revival* will help you remember the good stuff, and that your emotions will shift from drudgery to delight and your heart will experience renewal as you meditate on the unconditional love our Creator-Redeemer has lavished on you!

Warmest regards,
Lisa Harper
Women of Faith Ministry Director

Introduction

Awakening to God

In parts of the Christian tradition, the phrase "means of grace" has been used rather than "spiritual disciplines" precisely as a way to understand them as means (not needs) by which we open ourselves to the grace of God.

Steve Harper, author and former professor of spiritual formation, Asbury Theological Seminary[1]

Have you ever wondered what qualifies someone as an expert?

A recent study shows the number of hours required to achieve a certificate, bachelor's degree, or doctorate in prospective fields within the confines of a forty-hour work week. In the case of "un-degreed" fields, time spent performing activities that would lead to one being considered an expert was calculated. The results are startling. Consider the estimated amount of time required to become an expert in the following areas:

Neurosurgery: 42,240 hours

Economics: 26,880 hours

Culinary Arts: 13,440 hours

Sports: 9,600 hours

Knitting: 5,760 hours[2]

(Who would have thought becoming an expert knitter took so long?)

Would you consider yourself an expert in any area? Perhaps you've practiced a sport, played a musical instrument, or engaged in a particular task at work. Maybe you've honed your skills at singing, cooking, dancing, or training others.

It's no secret that whatever we practice for any significant length of time, we naturally become better at. But most of us can't become experts at something overnight. Studies show that, depending on the skill, it takes on average at least 10,000 hours of practicing something to become an expert.

This principle isn't true just for athletic activities and artistic expressions but for all of life—including our spiritual lives. For thousands of years, those within the church have committed themselves to practicing spiritual disciplines that help them connect with God and renew their desire for Him. At first many of these disciplines were challenging to those who began engaging in them, but over time they became well-worn paths for people and communities of faith to connect with God.

It's worth noting that over time the word *discipline* has collected a lot of baggage. All too often it's associated with reprimand or punishment, and that's one reason why these disciplines are sometimes referred to as "spiritual practices." And that is a great description, because not only do we get better at these disciplines with practice, but they help us grow closer to God. Each practice is a kind of fountain meant to refresh us, awaken us, cleanse us, and fill us. Through these practices we have the opportunity to connect with God and become more like Jesus.

These habits of holiness, which include prayer, study, silence, and more, aren't ends in and of themselves. They're never meant to be check-off-the-box-and-move-on kinds of activities. Rather, these practices are meant to be springboards to encourage us to live in daily dependence on God and become just a little more Christlike. We engage in these spiritual practices because we want to experience more of God and revival and transformation in our hearts.

Everyone is wired differently. So it's natural that you'll be attracted to or connect with some spiritual practices more than others. But as you dive into this study, may I challenge to you to try out each one, even if it's just for a single day? Some practices might feel a little uncomfortable or strange at first, but through them you just might find a way to connect with God that you've never experienced before. Also, consider which ones help you grow in dependence on God the most. You may discover that some awaken you to God in special and significant ways you didn't think possible.

My hope and prayer is that through this study you'll find yourself growing in your affection for God, becoming more Christlike in your attitude and actions, and finding a renewed zest for the life God has given you.

Blessings,
Margaret Feinberg

Celebrating Active Spiritual Practices

This first section
will introduce you
to active spiritual
practices. These holy
habits, including study of
Scripture, prayer, service,
fellowship, and more, call us
to engage our faith through
specific activities.

In the Bible God gives us revelations of Himself which lead us to worship, promises of salvation which stimulate our faith, and commandments expressing His will which demand our obedience. This is the meaning of Christian discipleship.

John Stott, Christian leader[1]

The Gift of Scripture

Throughout history, we find many men and women who were passionate about reading, studying, and memorizing Scripture, and their stories remain a source of inspiration for those of us on a journey of faith. Consider the following:

Fanny Crosby, a renowned hymn writer who was blind, learned to memorize the Bible as a child. By the time she was ten years old, she had committed the first four books of the Old Testament to memory, as well as the four Gospels. This may be one reason she was able to pen more than eight thousand hymns during the course of her lifetime.

William Wilberforce, famous for his role in abolishing slavery in England, was also known for his memorization of Scripture. Wilberforce would recite psalms while on walks—especially Psalm 119, the longest chapter in the Bible.

Corrie ten Boom, imprisoned in a concentration camp during World War II, noted that though they took away her Bible, they could not take away all the Scripture she had stored in her heart.

Each of these individuals discovered the incredible power of the Bible—the inspired Word of God. They knew and understood that the Bible is more than a collection of teachings or a recording of history; it is one of the primary tools through which God communicates with us and changes us.

Regularly reading, studying, and obeying Scripture will transform us.

In John 8:32, Jesus tells us, "And you shall know the truth, and the truth shall make you free." As we study God's Word, we're exposed to the truth of who God is and the work He longs to do in our lives. Reflecting on the truth of God's love, faithfulness, goodness, and justness, as well as His purposes for our lives, is one of the ways He works through us and begins changing our hearts to be more like His.

Regularly reading, studying, and obeying Scripture will transform us, because through the Bible we find encouragement and correction and are challenged to become more Christlike in every area of our lives. And when we use Scripture as the filter and the foundation through which we navigate opportunities and decisions in our lives, then God's Word becomes the standard for how we live.

The apostle Paul writes, "All Scripture is given by inspiration of God, and is profitable for doctrine, for reproof, for correction, for instruction in righteousness, that the man of God may be complete, thoroughly equipped for every good work" (2 Timothy 3:16–17). God uses the Bible to instruct, correct, and grow us. We don't study the Bible so we can win trivia quizzes, but so that we can become the kind of people through whom the love and goodness of God freely flows.

The way we approach reading the Bible matters. Before we ever open the great, big Book, we need to take a moment to ask God to meet us and reveal Himself in Scripture. It's as simple as asking God to speak to us through His Word. And as we read, we need to do so with a humble heart; this isn't about reading to simply gain more knowledge or to prove a point, but to encounter God and experience transformation.

As we read and study the Bible, we can know with confidence that God wants to speak to us, transform us, and make us more like His Son, Jesus.

While rewarding, reading the Bible can also be challenging, especially for those who are new to it. If you're struggling to read the Bible, it may be because of the translation that you're reading. Consider looking for a new translation—one that's much easier to digest, such as the New International Version or the New King James Version.

If reading in general is challenging for you, one idea is to consider listening to the Bible. We're blessed to live in a time when even if you can't read the Bible, you can still enjoy listening to an audio Bible. Listening to the Bible allows you to dive into the big story of God wherever you are.

It's also important to remember that some parts of the Bible are much more difficult to read than others. That's where a study Bible can come in handy and help unlock some of the history and context of the time in which the book was written. With a little background, passages that seemed strange and hard to read can become clear and accessible and applicable to your life.

Like any new spiritual practice, studying Scripture may seem hard at first, but know that with practice it will get easier, more enjoyable, and more exciting.

1. What role does studying Scripture currently play in your spiritual life? What's the greatest struggle you face when it comes to engaging in the spiritual practice of reading and studying the Bible?

2. Describe what it looks like for you to read or study Scripture in an average week.

3. Read **Philippians 4:8**. How does your perspective on life, others, and God change when you read the Bible frequently? How is your perspective on life, others, and God affected when you don't read the Bible for a while?

Even in Jesus' time, reading and studying Scripture was an esteemed practice. Each week, people traveled to their local synagogue to read the Torah (the first five books of the Old Testament) and some of the prophetic books out loud.

At the start of His ministry, Jesus traveled to the synagogue on Sabbath and stood to read from the book of Isaiah. The passage He read was a specific prophecy of the people's long-awaited Messiah.

4. Read **Luke 4:16–20**. How did Jesus fulfill the words of the prophet Isaiah and bring good news?

Scripture is one way God chooses to reveal Himself to us. Through Scripture, we catch a glimpse of God's character, unrelenting love, and faithfulness.

5. How did you first become aware of the good news of Christ? Did you first hear the good news through someone else or through reading Scripture?

Not only does Scripture give us a peek at God's heart, it transforms our hearts into Christ's likeness.

6. What do the following passages reveal about how the spiritual practice of reading and studying the Bible will affect your life? Place a star by the ones that you've found to be particularly true in your own life.

Joshua 1:8:

Psalm 119:9, 11:

Matthew 4:4:

Matthew 7:24–27:

James 1:25:

Immersing ourselves in God's Word also filters our thoughts and purifies our hearts. We are faced with a daily, ongoing battle for our hearts and minds. The things of this world tell us to live one way, but Scripture encourages us to become more and more like Jesus each and every day.

In Ephesians, Paul describes Christ's love for the church, which he compares to a relationship between a husband and wife. As the husband, Christ so loves His church that He sanctifies, cleanses, and presents her as pure. Through Jesus, we have been made perfect in God's sight, and like soap bubbling over dirty clothes, Scripture washes and renews our minds, drawing us back to God.

7. Read **Ephesians 5:25–27**. Why is it important for you to be washed by the cleansing of God's Word?

8. What steps can you take to make your time of personal Bible study more meaningful and impactful?

✤ Four Ways to
Practice Scripture Reading This Week

1. **Consider reading a large chunk of the Bible this week.** Read an entire gospel, such as Matthew or John. As you read, mark sections that you'd like to return to later and study in more depth.

2. **Choose one chapter of the Bible to read this week, such as John 17 or James 1, and study the passage in depth.** Use online tools, such as Bible word searches on biblegateway.com and commentaries, to learn as much as you possibly can about the chapter. Share what you discover with the group the next time you gather.

3. **Commit to memorizing at least one verse of the Bible this week.** You may want to choose a selection of Bible promises, such as Isaiah 40:29–31, or you may want to select a longer passage to commit to memory, like Psalm 139.

4. **If you've never read the Bible all the way through, consider committing to reading the entire Bible in a year.** Lots of free reading plans are available online, and with a commitment of only about four chapters per day, you can read the entire Bible in one year.

Digging Deeper

Read **Proverbs 30:5** and **Isaiah 40:8**. On the continuum below, mark how much of an impact the Bible plays in your everyday decision making. How does knowing that the Bible contains eternal truth affect the way you make decisions?

●——●

Little impact   **Great Impact**

Think often on God, by day, by night, in your business and even in your diversions. He is always near you and with you; leave him not alone.

Brother Lawrence, Carmelite monk[1]

The Gift of Prayer

When Great Britain's Prince William married Kate Middleton, their wedding attracted international media attention, with more than two billion people from around the world tuning in to watch the festivities.

The limited space at Westminster Abbey meant that only about 1,900 people were given a gold-stamped invitation to attend the wedding. Those who received invitations ran the gamut from the rich and famous to the commoner. Undoubtedly, some difficult decisions were made. For example, the president of France and his wife received an invitation, but the president of the United States and his wife did not. The invitations were exclusive because they were limited. Not everyone was invited to the celebration.

Yet the royal invitation by the King of Kings is different. He isn't constrained by space or limited by time. He doesn't need to make difficult decisions between national leaders and everyday citizens. Instead, He issues an invitation to each of us to come into His presence at any time, in any place, through the spiritual practice of prayer.

Put very simply, prayer is communicating with God, and we are invited to engage in a free, open, ongoing dialogue with Him throughout each and every day. Through prayer we can take our personal concerns to God, as well as the concerns of others. Through prayer we can express our adoration and affection for Him. We can make requests or petitions. We can confess our brokenness to God and ask for forgiveness. We can thank Him for His presence and His work in our lives. Through prayer we can learn to abide in Him.

Praying helps us make God our priority.

Prayer is a spiritual discipline we simply can't live without because prayer is one of the ways we open the door for God to transform us. Talking with God and taking the time to listen for His voice changes our desires so they are aligned with His will for our lives. Praying helps us make God our priority. The more we practice prayer, the more natural prayer will become. And when we don't know what to pray, we can cry out to God, who promises that the Holy Spirit will help us in prayer when we don't have the words to say (Romans 8:26–27).

However you choose to engage in the spiritual practice of prayer— by sitting down, standing up, kneeling, or walking—prayer is a gift and one that comes with great joy. Whether you've been praying for years or you're just learning to pray for the first time, growing in a life of prayer is a never-ending journey that takes you deeper into your relationship with God.

1. Describe a specific time when you experienced how your own prayers made a significant difference in your life.

2. Describe a specific time when you experienced the prayers of others making a significant difference in your life.

3. What do you imagine life would be like if you couldn't talk to God or have a close relationship with Him? How do you think it would affect your outlook and daily living?

Thousands of years ago, the church in Philippi withstood severe persecution from its unbelieving neighbors. In his letter to the Philippians, Paul encouraged the people to bring their anxieties, fears, and requests to God through prayer. He explained that God's peace would protect their hearts and minds like a military garrison protected a city.

4. Read **Philippians 4:6–7**. What situations do you face that are most tempting for you *not* to take to God in prayer? How does prayer impact the level of anxiety or worry you feel over a situation?

Throughout Jesus' earthly ministry, people in need surrounded Him. Yet despite the pressures and demands, Jesus took time to pull away and connect to God through prayer. Jesus recognized His tremendous dependence on God. He boldly declared that He couldn't do anything apart from God, and He only did what He saw His Father doing (John 5:19). One of the primary ways Jesus kept focused on God was through prayer.

5. What do the following passages reveal about the prayer life of Jesus—where He prayed, when He prayed, and who He prayed for?

Luke 9:18:

Luke 9:28:

Luke 11:1:

John 11:41–42:

The prayer life of Jesus revealed that He didn't only pray for Himself, but He also prayed for others. Jesus sometimes withdrew to pray by Himself; sometimes He took His friends. His prayer times varied. One of the keys to Jesus' prayer life was that He committed to pray regularly, and His prayer life often impacted His decisions.

6. Read **Luke 6:12–16**. What decisions did Jesus make after He prayed? What role does prayer play in your decision-making process?

There is no cookie-cutter formula when it comes to how to pray and what to say. God gives us freedom to express ourselves in prayer—whether that's walking, standing, kneeling, praying aloud, silently, with a group, for ourselves, or for others. Just as a relationship with your best friend would go sour if you stopped speaking, prayer invites us into a constant conversation with God so our relationship with Him can flourish.

7. In the space below, place a check mark by the types of prayer that you've tried. Then circle the ones that you've found most help you to engage in the spiritual practice of prayer.

   _____ Prayer walking, or walking through an area of a community to pray for the individuals who live and work there.

   _____ Praying the Bible by using passages of Scripture as prayers to God.

   _____ Popcorn prayers, or small prayers, that you pop out to God in the midst of your day.

   _____ Online prayers, when you post your prayer request on a website and invite others to join you in praying.

   _____ Praying repeated-breath prayers as you inhale and exhale to remind you of God's presence in each moment.

   _____ Praying during fixed times each day—praying at the top of the hour, spending each morning in prayer, or praying before a meal.

   _____ Sharing your prayer requests with a group and interceding on one another's behalf.

   _____ Memorizing and reciting liturgical prayers, such as the Lord's Prayer or the Aaronic Blessing.

   _____ Other:

8. What methods or practices have you found most helpful in learning to live a prayer-centered life?

What changes would you like to make in your life to grow in the spiritual practice of prayer?

✤ Four Ways to Practice Prayer This Week

1. **Commit to set aside five to ten minutes each day this week specifically for prayer.** Retreat from the busyness of life to talk to God with honesty and sincerity.

2. **Instead of speaking your prayers aloud or in your mind, choose to record your prayers in written form each day this week.** Pick up a notebook or journal and write down your words of thanks, requests, and adoration to God.

3. **Choose a passage from the Bible such as the Lord's Prayer (Matthew 6:9–13) or Psalm 23, and pray the passage for five minutes each day this week.** Ask God to help focus your heart and mind as you pray. Focus on each word as you speak them to God.

4. **Limit the length of your prayers each day this week.** Instead of using long-winded prayers, consider limiting your prayers to three words. Rather than thank God for this amazing day, simplify the prayer to, "Thanks for today." As you distill your prayers to their simplest form, reflect on what you're really saying to God and how much you are trusting Him.

Digging Deeper

Prayer may seem tedious or pointless at times—especially when the answers to our prayers aren't what we expect or when we expect them. Read **Colossians 4:12**. When have you found yourself wrestling in prayer? In what ways have you found prayer to be serious, hard work? What things in your life are most challenging to pray? What encourages you to keep on praying when others might give up?

> Nothing disciplines the inordinate desires of the flesh like service, and nothing transforms the desires of the flesh like serving in hiddenness. The flesh whines against service but screams against hidden service. It strains and pulls for honor and recognition.

Richard Foster, author of *Celebration of Discipline*[1]

The Gift of Service

Oswald Chambers committed his life to Christ after hearing Charles Spurgeon preach. He became a Baptist evangelist and served soldiers as a chaplain during World War I. When, in 1917, Oswald died from complications from an appendectomy, his wife, Biddy, was left a widow and single mom at the age of thirty-four. At the news of her husband's death, she sent a telegram to family and friends that announced, "Oswald is in His presence."

Biddy, who had worked as a stenographer and learned to write quickly using shorthand, had often used her talent to record her husband's sermons as he preached. After his death, Biddy decided to do something with all those notes of Oswald's sermons that she'd taken for years, so from them she put together more than fifty books, including the best-selling *My Utmost for His*

Highest. Each of the books bears the name Oswald Chambers, but only the initials of "B.C." for Biddy Chambers.

This sweet woman used her gift as a stenographer to serve her husband and, as a result, countless others around the world. The impact these works have had over the years is immeasurable. Biddy's willingness to serve in hiddenness—without recognition or public praise—highlights the important spiritual practice of service.

The spiritual practice of service grounds us in the truth that we weren't only designed for relationship with God.

Our faith in God isn't one just of belief but also of action. As followers of Christ, we're meant to use the gifts that God has given us for His glory and for the service of others. The spiritual practice of service grounds us in the truth that we weren't only designed for relationship with God; we were designed for relationship with others too.

We are meant to walk in the ways of Jesus, bringing freedom, healing, and justice to the world. We are meant to meet spiritual, relational, and basic physical needs. In responding to opportunities to serve others, we serve Christ and become more like Him.

Engaging in service as a spiritual practice invites us to consider not just when or how or who we serve but also the attitude with which we approach service. One can serve others for one's own gain—whether that's acknowledgement, fame, or a boost in reputation. But the service Christ calls us to is one in which we are ultimately serving an audience of One.

1. What are three gifts that you believe God has given you? What are three passions about the needs of others that God has given you (example: care for the homeless)? How are you using your gifts and passions to serve others right now?

2. What are three of the biggest lessons you've learned about God and others in the process of serving?

Often when we serve others, we become so filled with joy and excitement we can't help but share our deeds with those around us. However, Jesus warns us against this in Matthew 6. While Christ encourages service and righteous acts, He knows that boasting about our deeds is a stumbling block for some.

In Jesus' day the Pharisees (a group of legalistic Jews) carried out righteous acts in public, mainly to be noticed and praised by others. But Jesus reminds His followers that our reward is not from other people but from God. Instead, we are called to serve, pray, and fast in private, out of the fullness of transformed hearts.

3. Read **Matthew 6:1–4**. What challenges have you discovered as you've served others in hiddenness? How have you found the quote of Richard Foster that begins this lesson to be true in your own life?

Jesus not only taught about what it meant to serve others in private; He lived it. Through His life and ministry, we see Jesus choosing to serve others rather than be served.

4. Read the following passages. What do the following passages reveal about how Jesus served others? Place a star by the one that challenges or inspires you the most.

Matthew 8:1–4:

Matthew 14:34–36:

Matthew 15:32–39:

Mark 10:45:

John 13:3–5:

Jesus' disciples didn't quite understand the idea of servant leadership. At the request of John and James, their mother asked Jesus if her sons could sit at the right and left hands of the throne—two places of honor.

In response, Jesus described what greatness is through the eyes of God: not to be served, but to serve. His response must have shocked the disciples, who lived during a time when being a lord and master was respected and desired. But Jesus came to show how to live in the kingdom of God, which is starkly the opposite of the kingdom of men.

5. Read **Matthew 20:20–28** and **Matthew 23:11**. How does James and John's mother's definition of greatness compare to Jesus' definition of greatness? How is leadership related to service in Christ's kingdom?

In Isaiah 58, God reprimanded Israel for its outward religiosity, which was forced and fake, and reminded them that true righteousness is found in taking care of those in need. Jesus continued this idea in Matthew 25, when He told His followers that to serve others is to serve God.

6. Read **Matthew 25:34–40**. How does this passage affect your willingness to serve others? When have you most recently missed or refused an opportunity to serve Christ?

When we serve others, we may find ourselves running on fumes instead of serving out of the fullness of our hearts. In his letter to the Colossians, Paul reminded believers of the power of being filled up with Christ instead of serving out of our own energy.

7. Read **Colossians 1:24–29**. When in the last year have you served others with God's energy? When in the last year have you tried to serve others with your own energy? What difference have you seen between finding your strength in God versus using your own strength when serving others?

What are some of the greatest joys you've experienced from serving others? In what ways do you sense the Holy Spirit nudging you to serve others right now in your life?

✤ Four Ways to Practice Service This Week

1. **Call your local church office and ask if there are any immediate needs within the congregation that you can help meet.** Does anyone need to be visited in the hospital, delivered a hot meal, visited for an afternoon in a nursing home? Spend an afternoon being a servant to someone within your church community.

2. **Commit an entire day this week to being a servant to everyone in your household.** Go out of your way to meet every need you can, spoken and unspoken, with a cheerful attitude. As you go through the day, consider how cheerfully serving others affects them and you.

3. **Think of one person you know who has been going through a particularly difficult time.** Reach out to him or her and ask if you can serve in any way. If he or she doesn't have any specific suggestions, ask if you can bring a meal or go out to dinner together and serve through friendship, encouragement, and laughter.

4. **Get involved in your community.** What is one organization or outreach that you've always been interested in but never been involved in? Pick up the phone and find out how you can volunteer and contribute your time, money, and talents in service.

Digging Deeper

Read **Psalm 82:3**, **Isaiah 61:8**, and **Micah 6:8**. Prayerfully consider the areas in your workplace, home, or everyday life in which you have neglected to be a faithful servant or steward. Are there any areas in which you know that the direct or indirect result of your actions is causing harm to someone else or limiting their personal or financial growth? What can you do to bring justice to the situation and serve those who have been affected?

If you see your brother in need, it doesn't matter if you already gave somewhere else. You should be open to the idea of God using you to meet your brother's unexpected need.

Andy Stanley, pastor and author[1]

The Gift of Stewardship

A story is told of the time the famous evangelist D. L. Moody met a successful farmer. Proud of his hard work and financial success, the farmer boasted, "Everything you can see for miles is mine. Look to the south. Look to the north. It's all mine!"

"How much do you have in that direction?" Moody asked, pointing toward heaven.

While the farmer's wealth and success flourished on earth, Moody asked the most important question, reminding us that there are no luggage racks on a hearse. Earthly treasures are fleeting and temporal, but when we give to God, we invest in that which lasts forever and can never be taken away.

As followers of Jesus, we are called to hold our earthly treasures with an open hand and be cheerful and generous givers of our resources. The spiritual practice of stewardship comes from the word *steward*, which can be understood as one who is in charge of the affairs or property of another person. The idea of stewardship is similar to when people hire a manager to take care of their money or business. The manager does not own the business or money and can't spend it all as he or she pleases but is entrusted with the wealth of another.

Psalm 24:1 declares that everything is the Lord's—the earth, the world, and all who live in it. All is God's—including our wealth, treasures, and resources. We are merely stewards of all that God has entrusted to us.

As followers of Christ, we are called to daily take up our cross to follow Him. Our lives are not our own, but are God's, because we were purchased as a ransom for Christ's death. Just as Jesus wasn't selfish with His life, and He generously and lovingly gave it up for us, we are called to be generous stewards of every blessing God has given us.

God calls us to recognize that what we have isn't really ours—it's His!

Even if we don't have millions of dollars in the bank, God has still entrusted each of us with material possessions and resources, which may include families, relationships, ministries, businesses, time, and more. God calls us to recognize that what we have isn't really ours—it's His!—and we should rely on Him to determine how and when those resources are used.

When it comes to practicing stewardship, the real question isn't about the balance in your bank account or the square footage of your house; it's about the status of your heart. At its core, stewardship forces us to face the question of who really owns our lives: God or us?

1. What area of your life is the easiest and most joyful for you to practice generous stewardship?

2. In what area of your life are you most challenged in practicing generous stewardship?

Stewardship is not about who gives the most but about the heart behind the generosity. Practicing generous stewardship is a declaration of trust in God's provision. When we give cheerfully and generously, we are saying: "My life and everything in it is yours, God."

3. Read **Luke 21:1–4**. What do this woman's actions reveal about the practice of generous stewardship? What challenges you most about her actions?

The poor widow gave two small copper coins, the smallest coins of the time, yet Jesus commended her generosity—not because of the amount she gave, but because of the attitude of her giving.

The Bible tells of one young boy who had many reasons not to give what he had to Jesus—the small quantity of his lunch, the lack of freshness, the fear that if he gave it away, he wouldn't have anything to eat. Yet because of the boy's generosity, Jesus miraculously fed thousands. Jesus multiplied the boy's small offering as a testament to His power and provision—something He wants to do in our lives too!

4. Read **John 6:5–13**. Why do you tend to wrestle with giving and stewardship? What fears do you have?

5. When have you given something small—whether your time or a talent—and seen it used to accomplish much larger things?

Scripture repeatedly reminds us of our duty to be good stewards of the gifts God has lavished upon us.

6. What do the following passages reveal about the practice of stewardship?

Psalm 37:21:

Proverbs 3:9:

Matthew 25:14–30:

Romans 14:12:

2 Corinthians 9:11:

1 Peter 4:10:

What do you wish someone would have told you years ago about being a good steward?

Luke 16:10 says, "Whoever can be trusted with very little can also be trusted with much, and whoever is dishonest with very little will also be dishonest with much" (NIV). God calls us to be good, generous, and even cheerful stewards, from the littlest of gifts to the largest.

7. Read **2 Corinthians 9:7**. Some people say it's hard to outgive God. When have you found this to be true in your life? What did you learn from the experience?

8. In which areas of your life—time, talent, money, or other resources—do you sense the Holy Spirit nudging you to practice generous stewardship right now?

✤ Four Ways to Practice Stewardship This Week

1. **Whatever you've committed to give away financially, choose to increase your giving.** If you give away a percentage of your income, prayerfully consider increasing that number by 1 percent. If you give away a dollar amount each week, consider increasing that amount by 10–25 percent. Give until it feels really, really good.

2. **Keep a journal of how you spend twenty-four consecutive hours, in half-hour blocks.** Note how many hours a day you spend surfing the Internet, watching television, or mindlessly passing time. Prayerfully consider how you can reallocate that time toward more worthwhile activities, such as service, prayer, worship, or fellowship.

3. **Spend a few hours this week going through each room in your home and finding all the items that you've told yourself you needed but still sit unused.** Gather them and donate them to an organization where they can be used or sold.

4. **Take some time to reflect on Matthew 25:14–30 and the talents in your life that you may have buried.** What gifts has God given you that you're meant to steward well? How can you begin putting those gifts into action to bless, encourage, and serve others?

Digging Deeper

Read **Proverbs 11:24** and **Luke 6:38**. Why do you think generosity brings blessing? Why do you think stinginess brings lack? When have you seen these principles to be true in your own life? In what area of your life have you been most resistant to increasing your generosity? What's stopping you from giving more?

A journal is an aid to concentration, a mirror for the soul, a place to generate and capture ideas, a safety valve for the emotions, and a powerful tool for spiritual growth.

Ron Klug, author of *How to Keep a Spiritual Journal*

The Gift of Journaling

Personal notebooks and journals can be used for all kinds of great purposes. They can be used to capture sermon illustrations or insights, jot down notes from meaningful conversations, and record the highs and lows of each day.

Anne Frank, John Quincy Adams, Ben Franklin, and C. S. Lewis are just a handful of the people remembered through the words in their journals. Countless lives have been changed through their intimate and profound writings. In those pages, we catch glimpses of their hearts and minds, now published for everyone to glean from and enjoy.

With a little intentionality, the practice of journaling can have a profound impact on your life. Making time to write down your thoughts and ideas creates space for deeper and clearer thinking. As you write down your experiences and observations, you begin to see your life through a different lens, noting patterns and opportunities for reflection that you otherwise might have missed.

Through journaling we can record the specific ways that God is leading, nudging, and speaking into our lives through Scripture.

Journaling is a powerful tool for spiritual growth. The blank pages provide a safe place to ask God tough questions, wrestle through the mysteries of life, and record specific prayers. For some, journaling becomes writing prayers, an ongoing conversation with God that's recorded. Over time, it's possible to look back and see answered prayer, marks of spiritual growth, and testimonies of God's faithfulness. For others, journaling can help with Scripture memorization. Writing and rewriting a passage as well as regularly looking at it helps the words stick more readily.

Remember that journaling provides an opportunity to talk to God, honestly expressing your joys and heartaches—just as you are. For some of us, that will mean filling up pages each day. For others, it may be only a word or two or possibly a drawing or doodle. For still others, a poem or song may emerge. The practice of journaling provides yet another opportunity to meet with the most important person in your life— God. Don't wait another day to give this practice a try.

> Through journaling we can record the specific ways that God is leading, nudging, and speaking into our lives through Scripture.

1. Describe your own experience with keeping a journal or diary. How did you benefit from the practice?

2. Do you still journal now? If so, what keeps you going? If not, why did you stop?

3. Which of the following have you included in your diary or journal in the past?

_____ Praises   _____ Bible study insights

_____ Prayer requests   _____ Sermon insights

_____ Answered prayers   _____ Gratitude list

_____ Notes on personal growth   _____ Daily observations

_____ Bible verses   _____ Conversations with God

_____ Song lyrics   _____ Poetry

4. If you started the practice of journaling tomorrow, which of the elements listed above would you want to include? Why?

Journaling proves the opportunity to be fully yourself in the presence of God. The practice invites you to pour out your deepest thoughts, questions, heartaches, and joys to God.

Job is one man who never held back any punches when it came to his conversations with God. After losing almost everything, including his family, possessions, and health, Job continued to declare God's goodness in the midst of the storm raging around him.

5. Read **Job 19:23–25**. What are five things that you know to be true about God? Write them in the space below.

Many of the Psalms can be likened to journal entries from the life of David. Through his singing and songwriting, we are left with a rich legacy of prayers, praises, and laments to God. The Psalms reveal that David and the others who penned them were not afraid to express their doubts, frustrations, and anger to God. But they almost always ended with a word of thanksgiving or praise, a note that despite the challenges, God's goodness and faithfulness remain. Psalm 145 is a psalm of praise, declaring through poetry God's breathtaking majesty.

6. Read **Psalm 145**. Which is more meaningful for you, writing down what you know to be true about God or speaking it aloud? Which is more memorable? Why?

Psalm 22 is an individual lament psalm (as opposed to a communal lament, where a group of people cries out for help) in which David cries out for God's intervention in a distressing situation. The psalmist feels completely alone and abandoned by God and pours out his pain through writing. Jesus recited the beginning of this psalm while on the cross, expressing His deep agony and despair.

7. Read **Psalm 22**. What emotions are you most tempted to hold back from God? Does writing down what you're really feeling and thinking provide a healthy outlet for you to approach God, as a prayer? Why or why not?

8. What is the greatest challenge you face when it comes to the practice of journaling? How can you overcome it?

✤ Four Ways to
Practice Journaling This Week

1. **Select a favorite notebook and pen.** Using a notebook and writing utensil that you love can make journaling more fun. Begin by writing down the date. Reflect on which aspects of journaling from question 3 you want to include in your journal. Start writing. Don't worry about misspellings or errors. Simply allow yourself to be fully yourself with God through these pages. As you write, don't forget to take time to quiet yourself and listen for God.

2. **Make a goal to write in your journal every day this week.** As you write, consider what's helping you most to connect with God through prayer, study, and reflection. Be sure to be intentional to engage in these elements each day.

3. **Be creative. As you dive into the practice of journaling, consider how you can be most fully yourself in this space.** Maybe you'd like to use different colored pens to express how you're feeling or markers to create pictures of your prayers or heart before God. Maybe you'd like to include photos or scrapbooking elements.

4. **Journal online. Rather than keeping a print journal, consider recording a digital journal.** You may choose to keep your files on your computer and even share bits and pieces through a blog or online website. Always remember that journaling as a spiritual practice is not for sharing your words with others but is first and foremost for speaking with God.

Digging Deeper

As we look back at our lives, we can see God's fingerprints and faithfulness woven throughout. Journaling is a great way to record how God is moving in and through your life over a long period of time. Read **Psalm 78**. How does the psalmist record God's faithfulness over time? What are three examples of God's faithfulness in your life within the last year? What are three examples of God's faithfulness in your life within the last five years? How does remembering God's faithfulness encourage you in difficult situations?

The world is filled with reasons to be downcast. But deeper than sorrow thrums the unbroken pulse of God's joy, a joy that will yet have its eternal day. To set our hearts on this joy reminds us that we can choose how we respond to any particular moment.

Adele Ahlberg Calhoun, pastor and author[1]

The Gift of Celebration

What is your favorite part of Thanksgiving dinner?

The moist roasted turkey? The hearty mashed potatoes? The piping-hot rolls with melted butter? Perhaps it's the pecan, pumpkin, or apple pie. For most of us who live in America, Thanksgiving is a day set apart to feast and celebrate and is marked by a sense of gratitude.

Celebrating may seem like a minor addition to a list of spiritual practices, but have you ever considered that God calls us to throw parties and festivals and walk in the fullness of His joy? Jesus' arrival on earth was marked by joy and celebration, as noted when the angel declared, "I bring you good news that will cause great joy" (Luke 2:10 NIV). Jesus' first miracle was turning water into wine at a wedding, and His miracles that followed brought healing, wholeness, and celebration.

Those who follow Christ are called to walk in joy. Throughout the Old and New Testaments, the children of God are regularly called to feast and celebrate together in expressions of joy and to share our love of Him with others.

The practice of celebrating God grounds us in His faithfulness in the past, present, and future—it's no wonder that the ancient Israelites knew how to throw a great party in the form of a feast or festival. They understood that joy in the Lord is a source of strength and energy. The major feasts (or festivals) of the Old Testament included Passover, Unleavened Bread, Firstfruits, Pentecost (also known as the Feast of Weeks), Trumpets, Atonement, and Tabernacles (also known as the Feast of Booths). All these holidays brought the Jewish people together for worship, remembrance, and celebration of God. Together they recalled their common origin and kept the great story of God alive in their hearts.

The practice of celebrating God grounds us in His faithfulness in the past, present, and future.

Much like these ancient feasts, our holidays today call us to celebrate, even at moments in our lives when we may not feel like being joyful. Yet it's in those lean, difficult, painful moments that the spiritual practice of celebration is most important. The hard times give us the opportunity to remember God's faithfulness. When we choose to engage in the spiritual practice of celebrating, we don't simply forget our struggles; we make an active choice to celebrate God anyway.

Celebration and feasting is our expression of appreciation for all He has given us. Celebrating God reminds us that whatever we have is not the work of our hands but the work of our outrageously generous heavenly Father. By entering into those moments of abundance with joy—sometimes in the form of a delicious meal, dancing, or laughing with others—we remind ourselves of God's generosity to us. We are grounded in the truth that no matter what material possessions we may or may not have, we are rich through God's grace and love.

King David knew how to celebrate God. He found great joy in the presence of God and His faithfulness. In 2 Samuel, we read that after years of struggle, David finally captured Jerusalem, giving the Israelites not only a political headquarters but a religious one as well.

1. Read **2 Samuel 6:1–15**. Why was David rejoicing? How did David express his joy (hint: see verses 14–15)?

Giving ourselves over to celebration can make us feel vulnerable. We may risk being misunderstood or misinterpreted. Yet God calls us to find the fullness of our joy in Him.

King Saul's daughter, who was also King David's wife, Michal, watched her husband's boisterous celebration and burned with anger. Perhaps she was jealous of David's success or believed that her father could have done better. Either way, God did not bless Michal's anger.

2. Read **2 Samuel 6:16–23**. What was Michal's response to David's rejoicing (hint: see verse 20)? How did David answer Michal's complaint?

3. In what ways might the practice of celebrating feel uncomfortable, risky, or undignified to you?

One of the greatest celebrations of the Jewish people is Passover. This celebration traces back to the exodus of God's people from the wicked rule of Pharaoh in Egypt. After a series of mighty miracles, God instructed the Israelites to sacrifice a sheep or goat and apply the animal's blood on their doorframes—a sign that the angel of death should pass over their homes. That evening they feasted on roasted lamb, bitter herbs, and bread without yeast. They ate quickly, wearing their sandals as a sign of their readiness to leave Egypt.

4. Read **Exodus 12:1–30**. Why do you think God wanted the Israelites to commemorate or relive this event for generations to come? What did the original Passover reveal about the character of God and His love of His people?

The Passover became a communal and commemorative festival that continues to this day. People still gather together, including friends, family, and neighbors, to celebrate the holy holiday and to remember God's faithfulness. Even Jesus celebrated Passover, and it was during His final Passover celebration on earth that He revealed Himself more fully to His disciples.

5. Read **Matthew 26:17–27**. What parallels do you see between the lamb sacrificed for the protection of the people in Exodus and what Jesus was doing with His disciples on the eve of Passover?

Just as the Israelites were called to remember Passover each year, we are called to continue to celebrate God's continued faithfulness in our lives.

6. How does celebration impact your ability to remember the past, be present in the moment, or live with hopeful anticipation of the future?

7. Read **Zephaniah 3:17**. What is most meaningful to you about the idea that God celebrates over you? How can celebration help you not take yourself too seriously?

8. What is the greatest challenge you face when it comes to the practice of celebration? How can you overcome it?

✤ Four Ways to Practice Celebration This Week

1. **Reflecting on the passages in this week's study, including 2 Samuel 6:21–22 and Zephaniah 3:17, find a place in your home where you can be alone with God.** Make time to celebrate God with your voice and body. Consider thanking and praising Him aloud. Raise your hands. Maybe even add a twirl or two. Take time alone to worship God, freely and expressively.

2. **Select someone you know and celebrate God's work in his or her life.** Who in your life have you seen God moving through in profound or exciting ways? Invite the person over or out for a meal or ask him or her to participate in a favorite activity. Let the person know specifically how he or she has been an encouragement to you and the wonderful work you see God doing in his or her life. Remind that person how special he or she is to God and to you.

3. **Make time to visit the place where you feel most readily connected to God—whether in creation, in a chapel, in a small group, in an art studio, or in a chorus of worshipers.** Once you're there, ask God to fill you with His joy and presence. Spend time thanking Him and celebrating the work He is doing in your life.

4. **Take a look at the church calendar as well as your own calendar.** Select a holiday that you've overlooked or never known much about before and begin researching how you can celebrate it. Some suggestions include All Saints' Day, Pentecost, and Ascension.

Digging Deeper

Leviticus introduces the Jewish feasts and festivals to be celebrated by the Israelites. Because of their Jewish backgrounds, New Testament authors often make references to these celebrations. Read **Leviticus 23**. Fill out the chart below.

What does studying the feasts teach you about God's heart and character?

Passage	Feast/Festival	Passage	Significance in the New Testament
Leviticus 23:5		1 Corinthians 5:7	
Leviticus 23:6–8		1 Corinthians 5:7–8	
Leviticus 23:9–14		1 Corinthians 15:20–23	
Leviticus 23:15–22		1 Corinthians 12:13	
Leviticus 23:23–25		Matthew 24:30–31	
Leviticus 23:26–32		Matthew 27:51	
Leviticus 23:33–43		John 7:37–38	

Celebrating Inactive Spiritual Practices

The spiritual disciplines examined in this section are primarily inactive in that they don't call us to do something as much as to undo something and enter into the work that God does in and through us as we choose to do less, not more.

> Sabbath is not dependent upon our readiness to stop. We do not stop when we are finished. We do not stop when we complete our phone calls, finish our project, get through this stack of messages, or get out this report that is due tomorrow. We stop because it's time to stop.

Wayne Muller, Christian author and speaker[1]

The Gift of Sabbath

John Daggett worked as the superintendent of the San Francisco mint. In 1894, the mint produced only twenty-four coins. Knowing how few coins were made that year and that their value would one day skyrocket, John gave three of the precious dimes to his daughter, Hallie. He carefully instructed her to hold on to them because they'd be worth much more than ten cents one day.

After receiving the precious gift, Hallie stopped into one of her favorite soda shops and exchanged one of the dimes for a scoop of her favorite ice cream. Almost a century later, the ten-cent piece surfaced and sold for $34,100.

Today, only ten of these coins, known as 1894-S Barber dimes, exist in the world. They're some of the most sought-after coins of all time. That single scoop of ice cream ended up costing

Hallie more than she could have imagined, in part because she didn't understand the dime's real value.[2]

It seems silly to imagine trading something so precious, such as Hallie's coin, for something so fleeting, such as a scoop of ice cream. But, like Hallie, we all are tempted to choose the lesser above the invaluable whenever we allow our desires to get the best of us. Yet God has given each of us a spiritual practice to help keep our desires in check and realign our lives with Him regularly: the gift of rest, of Sabbath.

Sabbath reminds us that we are finite beings in the hands of an infinite God. It calls us to cease our toils and busyness for a day to declare that God is the One who holds everything in control, not us. Sabbath gives us a day to cease from our everyday demands and busyness to listen for God, to regain a sense of restfulness, and to allow God to rejuvenate our souls.

During Sabbath, we are called to live as set apart—creating a day that looks completely different from the other six days of the week. Like Hallie and her ice-cream cone, we may find ourselves tempted to trade in Sabbath for something that seems far better—such as getting ahead on our never-ending to-do lists. But choosing to stop and practice Sabbath gives us something priceless—namely, the opportunity to realign our full selves with God.

Sabbath reminds us that we are finite beings in the hands of an infinite God.

1. On the continuums below, record how tired you feel in each of the following areas of your life.

I feel well rested
emotionally.

I feel exhausted
emotionally.

I feel well rested
spiritually.

I feel exhausted
spiritually.

I feel well rested
physically.

I feel exhausted
physically.

I need a
Sabbath rest.

I celebrate
Sabbath regularly.

How much do you feel you could really use a Sabbath rest right now?

Sabbath reminds us that we are God's people. If God took time out of creation to rest, how much more do we, as finite beings, need to do the same? Sabbath serves as a needed reminder that we are part of God's kingdom—a place without clocks, schedules, and stress.

2. Read **Genesis 2:1–3**. How is the Sabbath day different from every other day of creation? What does God's participation in the Sabbath reveal about our invitation to participate in the Sabbath?

A command to honor the Sabbath is included as one of the Ten Commandments given to Moses on Mount Sinai. The fourth commandment calls us to remember the Sabbath.

3. Read **Exodus 20:1–17**. What specific directives are given for the Sabbath? What do the directives for the Sabbath reveal about God's character and love?

Isaiah 58 includes instructions to the Israelites on how to perform righteous acts as God intended. The Israelites at the time were performing selfish and self-righteous fasts but were completely ignoring the command to honor the Sabbath.

Just as fasting, prayer, silence, and other practices can be tainted, Sabbath is another area in which humans have manipulated God's original intention. God designed Sabbath, not as a day to finish everything we didn't get done during the first six days of the week, but as a day to fill our time with His presence and invest in our relationship with Him.

4. Read **Isaiah 58:13–14**. What promises are given to those who honor the Sabbath?

5. Have you ever attempted to enter into Sabbath rest? What did the day look like for you? What were the day's greatest joys and challenges?

6. What prevents you from celebrating the Sabbath each week?

While initially designed to be a delight to God's people, Sabbath was quickly turned into a legalistic exercise for the Jewish people. The enjoyment and delight was squeezed out and replaced with rules. But Jesus went out of His way to demonstrate and teach that the Sabbath was a gift for the people of God, not a burden. Jesus repeatedly broke the Sabbath laws in order to do good and bring healing to others.

7. Read the following passages. What did Jesus specifically do on the Sabbath?

Mark 3:1–6:

John 7:23:

John 9:14:

In Jewish tradition, Sabbath begins at sundown on Friday and extends until sundown on Saturday. As Jewish families begin shutting down their work and busyness on Friday evening, they set an empty chair in the room: an ongoing reminder of God's presence, protection, and providence in their lives.

8. Read **Hebrews 4:9–11**. What changes do you need to make in your life to practice the Sabbath regularly? How do you think regularly observing the spiritual practice of Sabbath rest would impact your spiritual life and relationship with God?

✤ Four Ways to Practice Sabbath This Week

1. **Tackle daily projects the day before the Sabbath.** Whatever day of the week you choose to celebrate the Sabbath, know that it's going to take preparation. You may want to prepare a meal in a slow cooker so you don't have to cook and clean on the Sabbath. You may want to go ahead and do laundry or pick up the living room or yard the day before. Try to remove as much work and chores as possible from your Sabbath day.

2. **Select one or two spiritual practices to engage in on the Sabbath.** Set aside time for prayer, Bible study, solitude, silence, or some of the other practices explored in this study.

3. **Make a list of life-giving activities.** Sabbath rest isn't just about taking a long nap but should include activities that restore your soul. The list may include artistic expressions, engaging in a sport, or sipping iced tea on the back porch with a friend. Engage in personally restorative activities—just remember to do so at a leisurely, restful pace.

4. **Remember that the Sabbath isn't about making a list of what to do or what not to do; it is meant to be a day set apart from the others as holy.** This is a day to express our adoration of God and experience His adoration of us. This is a day to be refreshed. What you choose to do on the Sabbath may be very different from what someone else chooses to do. Always extend grace, compassion, and love when it comes to any differences of perspective.

Digging Deeper

Sabbath reminds us that we are not in control of our lives but that God holds everything together. When we take a break and carve out time to practice the Sabbath, we can rest assured that everything is under God's control.

Read **Ezekiel 20:12, 20**. Why do you think God gave the people the Sabbath? How does keeping the Sabbath set you apart from others who don't keep the Sabbath? What difference do you notice in your life when you regularly celebrate the Sabbath?

The beginning of prayer is silence.

Mother Teresa, Christian nun[1]

The Gift of Silence

All too often silence makes us

uncomfortable. The blank spaces, whether in our conversations or even on this page, cause us to wonder if something has gone wrong, if we're missing something. Our natural tendency is to fill in the space, to eliminate the silence.

The writer Henri Nouwen once observed:

Over the last few decades we have been inundated by a torrent of words. Wherever we go we are surrounded by words: words softly whispered, loudly proclaimed, or angrily screamed; words spoken, recited, or sung; words on records, in books, on walls, or in the sky; words in many sounds, many colors, or many forms; words to be heard, read, seen, or glanced at; words which flash off and on, move slowly, dance, jump, or wiggle. Words, words, words! They form the floor, the walls, the ceiling of our existence.[2]

Nouwen wrote these words more than thirty years ago. Since then, the development and availability of the Internet has made words even more prevalent, especially the constant barrage that comes from social media outlets. As followers of Jesus, we know that God is with us at all times, but how often do we take time simply to be with God and listen for His voice?

In the bustle of chores, errands, and work, often we don't realize how much we're surrounded by noise; our lives are rarely silent. And often we fear silence because without all those distractions, we are confronted with feelings and thoughts we've been trying to run from—worry, anxiety, doubt, and fear. Silence tends to bring these emotions to the surface, but rather than try to hide them from God, we can now recognize them and take them to God in prayer, asking for the comfort and guidance only He can give.

> The practice of silence isn't about removing all the excess sounds from our lives as much as it's about removing the excess distractions.

The practice of silence isn't about removing all the excess sounds from our lives as much as it's about removing the excess distractions that pull our attention away from God. Through silence we accept the invitation to just be with God. Silence provides the opportunity for reflection and contemplation, and in silence we have the comfort of praying without even using words, communicating with God by simply enjoying His presence and knowing He is near.

In silence, we give time for God to speak and for us to respond. Prayers naturally arise from our lips and hearts. The words of the Bible come alive in a whole new way. In silence. we create space to enjoy God's presence and adhere to the words of the psalmist, "Be still, and know that I am God" (Psalm 46:10).

1. Describe a time when you have felt close to God without saying anything at all. What was most striking about the experience?

2. Silence stands in stark contrast to the noise of everyday life. Set a timer for five minutes and enter a time of deliberate silence to seek God. What stirred in your heart during this time of silence?

3. When you approach God in prayer, what percentage of time do you give to speaking versus listening? What makes giving time to listen to God so challenging?

Psalm 131 is a Song of Ascents written by King David—part of a series of psalms that exalt and praise God. Scholars believe that Jewish priests would recite these psalms as they walked the steps into the inner courtyard of the temple as a way to prepare their hearts to meet with God. Other scholars believe these songs were sung as people made a pilgrimage into Jerusalem, the Holy City.

4. Read **Psalm 131:1–2**. What are some of the challenges you face when you try to quiet your soul?

5. What are some effective ways you've found to respond to the distractions you sense when practicing silence?

When we pause our lives and silence our voices, we make room for God to speak. However, sometimes God doesn't speak as quickly, loudly, or clearly as we would like. In times of silence, we may find ourselves simply waiting on God.

6. On the continuum below, mark how well you feel that you wait on the Lord.

I wait on the Lord well.   **I struggle to wait on the Lord.**

Waiting on the Lord is a difficult task. However, Scripture encourages us that even in the midst of the waiting, God has not abandoned us. We can find rest and salvation in God while we wait.

7. Read **Psalm 62:1–8**. What did David discover to be true about God as he waited in silence?

8. According to the passages below, what are some of the promises and rewards of those who learn to wait on the Lord?

Isaiah 30:15:

Isaiah 40:30–31:

How do you think incorporating the practice of silence into your spiritual journey can help you grow in your relationship with God?

✤ Four Ways to Practice Silence This Week

1. **Each day this week carve out time to be with God in silence.** Begin
   with a timer set for one minute and each day add an additional minute.
   During the silence, consider reflecting on Psalm 46:10 or another
   meaningful passage.

2. **Consider making silence a fifteen-minute vacation during your day.**
   Turn off your phone and all electronic devices. Find a quiet room in your
   house or a peaceful spot outside and simply enjoy God's presence in your
   life. Offer up words of thanks in the silence.

3. **Consider going on a retreat to a quiet place for a set-apart time of
   silence.** Some retreat centers offer silent retreats in which even meals
   are eaten without speaking. Ask God to speak to you during this time.

4. **Challenge yourself to go an entire day without the radio or
   television.** Instead, fill those times with silence, asking God to quiet your
   heart as you focus your attention on Him alone.

Digging Deeper

The Israelites were no strangers to silence and waiting on God. But God
was always listening. In the midst of the Israelite's four hundred years of
slavery in Egypt, God heard their cry and sent Moses to free them from
Pharaoh's oppression and call them into the promised land.

Read **Exodus 2:23–25**. What is something you've been praying about
and have heard only silence in return? How does the story of the Israelites
in Exodus restore your hope?

To be left alone with Him is a foretaste of heaven.

Lettie B. Cowman, author of *Streams in the Desert*[1]

The Gift of Solitude

When was the last time you dreamed about getting away from it all?

Perhaps you saw one of those catchy vacation ads on television, from a website that promises booking your next getaway is just a click away. Or maybe you saw an ad for a cruise ship that offered an image of a family on a remote beach, away from all the demands and noisiness of everyday life. How appealing and luxurious that sounds!

But how often do we really do it? And what do we really hope to gain from it?

In our modern world, the idea of getting away from it all is often heralded, but most of us find it hard to do. The practice of solitude invites us to experience more than just getting away from all the noise of our lives. It's more than a vacation or weekend getaway to the mountains. Solitude is the act of withdrawing for the purpose of being alone to seek God through prayer, study, journaling, and listening to Him.

The Bible is chock-full of people who encountered God through solitude. Moses was alone when he stumbled upon a burning bush. Elijah was alone when God whispered to him on the side of a rocky mountain. Mary was alone the night the angel delivered the message of her pregnancy.

Solitude is a door through which we step away from the busyness of life and seek God so that we may be recharged and energized and find our hearts and minds more aligned with Him and His will for our lives. God often uses solitude, coupled with silence, to work in our hearts and prepare us for service. Throughout Jesus' busy ministry, He regularly retreated from everyone and used the practice of solitude to pray, listen to God, seek direction, receive wisdom, and be refreshed. If Jesus needed times of solitude, how much more do we?

Solitude is the act of withdrawing for the purpose of being alone to seek God through prayer, study, journaling, and listening to Him.

1. Where do you go to find solitude? When are you most aware of your need for the practice of solitude?

2. Does anything about the practice of solitude make you hesitant or fearful? If so, describe your concerns.

Solitude can be terrifying for even the most introverted among us. But there is nothing to fear when you are carving out time with God. Solitude allows space for the Holy Spirit to dig into the deep recesses of our hearts, offer us freedom, and lavish us with grace and love.

3. Read **Song of Solomon 2:13**. When was the last time you sensed God beckoning you to spend time with Him? How did you respond?

Imagine your relationship with a dear friend or spouse. What would happen if you didn't speak to him or her or see that person for weeks on end? You probably wouldn't be as close or intimate as you once were. In the same way, God beckons us to spend time with Him and grow in our relationship with Him.

4. What happens when you get too busy to take time to be alone with God? How does skipping time with God affect your attitude and outlook on life?

Jesus understood the importance of unplugging from the world and carving out time to be alone with God. So much so that each of the gospel authors recorded instances of Jesus celebrating the practice of solitude.

5. What do each of the following passages reveal about how Jesus practiced solitude throughout His earthly ministry?

Matthew 14:23:

Mark 1:35:

Luke 5:16:

John 6:15:

What single issue in your life do you think would improve if you practiced solitude more often?

Elijah, an Old Testament prophet, experienced a special encounter with God while practicing solitude. After being on the run from an evil king and queen, Elijah found himself alone on a mountainside, waiting to hear from God. Yet the way God revealed Himself is both surprising and breathtaking.

6. Read **1 Kings 19:11–18**. How did God reveal Himself to Elijah? How do you think the practice of solitude can build intimacy with Jesus and maturity in your walk with Him?

7. What have you found works for you when it comes to carving out times for solitude in the midst of your weekly schedule?

8. What changes do you need to make in your life in order to practice solitude regularly?

✤ Four Ways to Practice Solitude This Week

1. **Select a favorite place to be with God for at least thirty minutes of solitude this week.** Choose your favorite recliner, park bench, or rocking chair. Talk to God—even aloud. Dedicate the time to praying, singing, writing, and simply being with God.

2. **Be intentional about setting apart at least a half day in the upcoming months to practice solitude.** Find a time on your calendar when you can get away to a quiet place, whether it's a spiritual retreat center, monastery, or local hotel for a more intense time of practicing solitude. Use the time to quiet your heart and to pursue God through petition, worship, adoration, and thanksgiving, as well as silence.

3. **Solitude invites us to be with God.** One of the ways we can do this is by studying and reflecting on the Bible in our time with Him. This week, carve out fifteen minutes to be alone with God. As you sit, read Revelation 8:1–5 and imagine yourself in the scene, joining in the worship of God.

4. **Make the time you spend in the shower a time of solitude.** Each time you take a shower or bath, be intentional about seeking God, praying, and praising God. As you bathe, be reminded that God is washing you new each day and transforming you into His likeness.

Digging Deeper

Solitude offers time away from crowds and what others think of us and helps us be grounded in who we are in God's eyes.

Read the passages below and fill in the blanks with descriptions about who God says you are. How does seeing yourself as God does transform the way you think and address others?

John 1:12: I am _____

John 15:15: I am _____

Romans 6:6: I am _____

Romans 8:2: I am _____

2 Corinthians 5:17: I am _____

Ephesians 1:4: I am _____

Ephesians 1:7: I am _____

One of the greatest fallacies of Christian faith, and actually one of the greatest acts of unbelief, is the thought that spiritual acts and virtues need to be advertised to be known.... Secrecy, rightly practiced, enables one to place the public relations department entirely in the hands of God.

Dallas Willard, pastor and author[1]

The Gift of Secrecy

When was the last time you posted something on Facebook, Twitter, Pinterest, or another online site to share something about your life? How many times have you posted this week?

It's fascinating to see what people share about themselves online—what they've had for lunch, a photo of their pet or kids playing in the backyard, an update on how their date is going—while they're still on the date!

Social media provides an incredible opportunity to connect with others throughout the day, but it doesn't come without some unhealthy temptations. We can begin to feel that every moment of our lives needs to be documented. The process of constantly taking photos and uploading updates means we're not fully present and we're missing some of the moment. A second temptation is to begin to cultivate a persona we want to share with the world that isn't true. But one of the biggest temptations is that we can begin to feel that we're not validated or that an experience isn't real until we've shared it with someone else. We can easily cross the line into oversharing.

Staying constantly plugged in can keep us distracted and increasingly unplugged from God. Yet Scripture calls us to plug into God and not worry about the accolades and attention of others. In the life of Jesus, we see what it means to live as a master of surprise and secret-keeping.

The practice of secrecy calls us to follow Jesus by demonstrating hiddenness and anonymity in our spiritual lives.

Jesus was very deliberate about when and with whom He shared details about God's kingdom and the surprising twists that unfolded through His life, death, and resurrection. And though Jesus was very clear that we're called to share the good news with others, He was also concerned with our ability to keep a secret.

Jesus recognized something that we are sometimes slow to realize: when we perform acts so we can feel good or receive accolades, then we reveal that our service is really all about us, not God.

In the Sermon on the Mount, Jesus made it clear that we are never to practice our good works or righteousness in front of others for the purpose of being seen by them. Rather, we're to practice such acts, including prayer, fasting, and giving, in secret so that God alone may see them. Jesus didn't just teach this; He demonstrated it throughout His life. He frequently urged people not to reveal His identity. He often retreated to quiet places to get away. Jesus walked in humility and utmost dependence on His Father.

The practice of secrecy calls us to follow Jesus by demonstrating hiddenness and anonymity in our spiritual lives. This means that when we give or when we serve, we should be intentional about *not* letting others know what we've done or bragging to others afterward. The practice of secrecy isn't about being dishonest or covert but is simply about remaining humble and resisting the urge to intentionally make our good works known.

As we practice secrecy, we find our desires for fame and acclaim begin to wither. Rather than compete for attention, we can embrace peace and contentment out of the hidden riches of our relationship with God. In the process, our value shifts from what others say about us to what God thinks about us.

1. On a scale of 1 to 10, how good are you at keeping a secret? What's the best secret you've ever been a part of?

2. How does the practice of secrecy expose your own need for approval and accolades?

Secrecy challenges us to put our own desires for praise and approval aside, and seek ultimate approval from God alone. In the same way, the practice of secrecy reminds us that not everything is public knowledge.

Much of what is told to us in private should stay private. Secrecy challenges our desire to know everything, to gossip, or to spread rumors.

3. When was the last time someone betrayed a confidence of yours? What did it feel like? How did the betrayal impact your relationship with the person?

Jesus understood our desire for recognition but reminded us that our lives are not our own. He challenged us to do things in secret to praise God alone instead of doing deeds to lift ourselves up. Secrecy reminds us that not everything we do needs to be in the spotlight and we shouldn't expect rewards.

Jesus confronted the Pharisees' thinking at the time. (The Pharisees were a group of self-righteous religious leaders who lifted themselves and their holiness up for their own benefit.)

4. Read **Matthew 6:1–21**. In the space below, make a list of all the areas in which Jesus calls us to practice secrecy. How does the practice of secrecy in each of these areas increase your dependence on God alone?

Jesus was the perfect example of someone who practiced outrageous generosity and offered extravagant gifts of healing and freedom but never looked for a reward. Instead, He served an audience of One.

5. Read the following passages and fill in the chart below.

Passage	Who Jesus Addressed	What Jesus Instructed Them Not to Tell
Mark 1:40–44		
Mark 9:2–9		
Luke 8:40–56		

In each case, why do you think Jesus instructed the people not to tell others what had happened?

6. Read **Philippians 2:3**. How does practicing secrecy free you from the opinions of others?

7. On the continuum below, mark who is easier to seek praise and approval from. In what areas of your life do you find it easier to seek God's approval? In what areas of your life do you find it more difficult to seek God's approval?

It's easier to seek approval from others.   **It's easier to seek approval from God.**

8. What changes do you need to make in your life in order to practice secrecy? How do you think the spiritual practice of secrecy would impact your spiritual life and relationship with God?

✤ Four Ways to Practice Secrecy This Week

1. **This week do something outrageously kind or generous for someone without letting them know it was done by you.**

2. **Be a safe place for someone this week.** As you spend time with someone who is sharing vulnerably, commit that you will keep his or her confidences and share only what you've learned with God through prayer.

3. **Resist being the hero or one-upping people this week.** Throughout conversations, refrain from telling stories in which you're the hero or that highlight your good deeds. If people share something that happened to them, avoid one-upping their story with one of your own.

4. **Spend time with God and ask Him to reveal something to you through Scripture or prayer that you will keep between just the two of you.** Practice secrecy between you and God for the upcoming week.

Digging Deeper

Read **John 3:30**. How can you make yourself less, putting God and others above you in your home? In your workplace? With your friends? At your church? Copy John 3:30 on a note card or Post-It note and place it in your home, car, or workplace. As you see the verse, remind yourself to do God's work in secrecy, not for earthly praise and approval but for God's glory.

At first fasting intensifies hunger; then it quiets both the heart and body; and then increases a desire that can rightly be called "homesickness."

Dan B. Allender, PhD, Christian therapist, author, and professor[1]

The Gift of Fasting

Do you have a favorite celebrity chef?

Perhaps you enjoy watching Gordon Ramsay, Anthony Bourdain, or Bobby Flay on TV. Maybe you prefer Mario Batali, or Emeril Lagasse. Whichever chef or cooking show you prefer, there's no doubt that food has become more than a source of nourishment or comfort; it has also become a source of entertainment.

In spite of all the tempting food-based television shows, clever cooking tricks, and scrumptious recipes, one of the spiritual disciplines that can stir our hunger for God most is fasting. But fasting isn't just about abstaining from food. (That's dieting.) Instead, fasting is the act of laying down an appetite—whether for food, shopping, watching TV, or more—and allowing ourselves to experience what our souls hunger for most: Jesus.

When teamed with prayer, the spiritual practice of fasting can pack a powerful punch for transforming the lives of followers of

Christ. Scripture records dozens of examples in which fasting, coupled with prayer, was a way for people to refocus their hearts on God. As we fast, we exchange our physical needs for spiritual ones. As we abstain from one thing, we seek to be filled with God's Word, prayer, and fellowship with Him.

Fasting regularly can help us deepen our relationship with God. When we abstain from something—whether food or something else clouding our lives—we are declaring that God is in full control of our lives. Fasting helps clear the clutter that settles into our minds and hearts.

Fasting helps clear the clutter that settles into our minds and hearts.

Fasting takes many forms. Some people fast for a meal or a day. Some people fast from solid foods or specific foods like meat. During the season in the church calendar known as Lent—the forty days before Easter—many people fast from an activity that distracts them from God.

Whatever the fast, the purpose of fasting is to focus our attention on God more fully. Fasting is never about just getting what we want from God; it is an act that's meant to be paired with prayer and humility as we intentionally seek God and His will for our lives as we learn to fully rely on Him.

Scripture reminds us, "Man shall not live by bread alone, but by every word that proceeds from the mouth of God" (Matthew 4:4). When we fast, we allow God to fill our hearts, souls, and minds with His presence.

1. People often choose to fast from many different things—not just from food but from particular types of food or beverages, social media, technology, and more. What kinds of fasts have you attempted? What did you learn from them?

Many followers of Christ give something up as a fast during specific periods of time to prepare their hearts for a season, such as Advent (the weeks leading up to Christmas) or Lent (the forty days before Easter). In fasting from something during these time periods, we allow more space in our lives to take hold of Jesus Christ.

2. For some people (including those with medical conditions), abstaining from food may not be possible. How else can fasting be expressed as a discipline?

Fasting does not need to be solely associated with food. Instead, the idea of fasting is to let go of the earthly hold something has in our lives and remind us of our complete reliance on God. For some, giving up their cell phone, Facebook, or television for a time is what they need to remind themselves to take hold of Christ and God's promises. Others may want to give up caffeine or secular music for a time.

Whatever God is calling us to fast from, the point is to declare our trust in God as He renews and sustains our hearts.

3. Read **Matthew 6:16–18**. What specific instructions does Jesus give regarding fasting? What do you think is the purpose of each instruction?

How does God respond to secret acts of righteousness?

What do you think pleases God when we choose to fast?

Scripture records many people, including Jesus, fasting for various reasons and amounts of time. One example is found in the book of Daniel. For twenty-one days, Daniel ate only fruits, vegetables, unleavened bread, and water. This partial fast has encouraged many Christians to begin the Daniel Fast as a way to kick off the New Year.

4. Fill in the chart below.

Passage	Who Fasted	What Was Abstained From	Length of Fast	Result of Fast
1 Samuel 1:1–20				
Esther 4:13–17; 8:4–14				
Matthew 4:1–11				
Acts 9:1–18				

Not only do the amount of days and what is abstained from vary, so do the purposes of each fast in Scripture. God may call us to fast from things for many reasons. It is important to remind yourself that fasting from something encourages you to lay hold of something else and does not guarantee the response from God that you may be looking for.

5. Look up the following passages and note the purpose of each fast.

Deuteronomy 9:18, 25:

Ezra 8:21–23:

Ezra 10:6:

2 Samuel 12:15, 16, 22–23:

Judges 20:26–28:

Psalm 35:13:

Acts 13:1–3:

6. Which of the purposes listed above would you be willing to fast for?

While it is an important spiritual practice, fasting is not for everyone. Scripture offers several warnings that remind us that fasting doesn't matter unless the heart behind the discipline is engaged.

7. What warning do the following passages provide regarding fasting?

   Isaiah 58:

   Luke 18:9–14:

   Which of these warnings is most significant to you? Why?

8. What is the greatest challenge you face when it comes to the practice of fasting? How can you overcome it?

✤ Four Ways to Practice Fasting This Week

1. **Talk to a health-care professional.** Before you consider fasting from any type of food, talk to your medical provider to ensure that abstaining from food will not damage your body in any way or have adverse health effects. This is essential. Based on the response of your medical provider, choose how to best engage in the practice of fasting.

2. **Give up a meal one day this week.** Choose one meal to skip in order to set apart the time and energy to pursue God through prayer, study, and worship. This may seem like a small act, but it's significant to God and can be a great launching pad for focusing your attention on Him.

3. **Consider spending a day eating only vegetables, fruit, and grains— no meat or delicacies like fried food.** This type of fast, often referred to as a Daniel Fast, allows you to consume as many fruits and vegetables as you need. Like all fasts, the purpose is not for dietary restriction but for connecting with God.

4. **Abstain from an activity that distracts you from God.** What activity is consuming the extra time in your day that you could be spending with God? Everyone's activity may be different. Maybe it's television, movies, gaming, social media, surfing the Internet, texting, or puttering around the house. Whatever your activity, consider giving it up for a day this week to set apart time to read, study, and worship.

Digging Deeper

Read **Psalm 42**. What themes of hungering and thirsting for God emerge from this passage? In what ways have you experienced God satisfying your deepest hungers and needs? How does denying your desires create a greater desire for God in your life?

We have an uncanny ability to accumulate things that are not essential to living, yet we lack the practice of releasing the acquired junk when it no longer serves a purpose.

Jeff Shinabarger, founder of Plywood People[1]

The Gift of Simplicity

Teresa of Avila believed in practicing simplicity throughout her life. As the founder of the Barefoot Carmelites, she started sixteen nunneries and fourteen convents. Instead of creating a lavish life of excess, Teresa intentionally chose simplicity. Her nuns' outfits were made of coarse brown fabric. The veils featured no folds. They slept on straw. They kept their hair short. Teresa lived in a tiny room without furniture and only straw for a bed and sackcloth for covers.

Upon her death, a slip of paper was found that read, "He who has God lacks nothing. God alone suffices."[2]

The basic lifestyle was meant to help Teresa and the women she led keep their focus on God. While most of us won't live lives of such extreme austerity, Teresa's life challenges us to reflect on the areas in our own lives in which we can become more dependent on God through the practice of simplicity.

Simplicity may mean eating more simply, dressing in less extravagant ways, downsizing what we own, removing unnecessary complications from our lives, or cutting away our preoccupation with getting more stuff. As we detach ourselves from the things of the world, we cling even tighter to the cross. Gratitude abounds and joy overflows.

Simplicity dares us to hold loosely our time and treasure as we let go of attachments and allow God to move in us and through us, flooding us with the freedom to give. This practice asks us to untangle our lives so that we can become focused on God as our source of strength and fulfillment. Simplicity replaces our need for "more, more, more" with a sense of "give, give, give," trusting in God as our Provider.

We simplify with the intention of placing God on the throne of our hearts. When we do, we find ourselves fulfilling Jesus' command to seek first His kingdom and righteousness (Matthew 6:33) and loving the Lord with our whole hearts, souls, minds, and strength (Mark 12:30).

As we detach ourselves from the things of the world, we cling even tighter to the cross.

1. In which of the following areas have things grown overly complicated in your life? Place a check by each one. Which of those that you checked do you most long to simplify?

_____ Schedule   _____ Relationships

_____ Daily commitments   _____ Upkeep of home

_____ Family   _____ Work

_____ Finances   _____ Other

2. How have you seen your identity as a child of God impacted by leading a complicated or cluttered life?

Jesus and those who followed Him were no strangers to living simply. The Israelites believed that the Messiah would come as a mighty king or strong warrior; instead, Jesus came in a manger, wearing no crown and carrying no sword. Jesus not only taught simplicity; He lived it.

3. Read **Mark 1:1–19**. How did each of the following people practice simplicity early in their ministries? How are you challenged by these men's simple living?

John the Baptist (1:4–6):

Jesus (1:12–13):

The disciples (1:16–20):

Jesus called His followers to live simply and pack light to encourage their reliance on God and so they could engage directly with those to whom they were ministering. Jesus reminded the disciples that their job was not to be self-sufficient but to trust God as their Provider.

4. Read **Luke 9:1–6**. Why did Jesus call the disciples to practice simplicity in their service? How does having less affect your ability to depend on God more?

Many times we may find ourselves sitting on the fence between trusting God and taking care of things ourselves. While trusting God as our Provider sounds great, we may ask ourselves those "What if" questions: *What if I lose my job? What if ends don't meet? What if there is an unexpected injury?* Jesus reminds us that worrying adds nothing to our lives; instead, we are called to practice trust each day.

5. Read **Matthew 6:25–26**. How does having more tend to impact the level of anxiety, stress, and worry in your life? How have the beliefs that "bigger is better" and "more is better" impacted your life?

As we simplify our lives, we can rely on God to provide for us. One way to do so is to focus our attention on the things of God instead of on the things of this world.

6. Read **Colossians 3:1–2**. In your efforts to practice simplicity, do you tend to struggle more with areas of commitments or areas of possessions? Explain.

7. How does simplicity empower you to exhibit childlike trust in God? What keeps you from living a life marked by simplicity?

8. What do you sense God is calling you to downsize in your life so that you can practice simplicity?

✤ Four Ways to
Practice Simplicity This Week

1. **Make time to slow down this week.** One of the ways we can practice simplicity is simply by slowing down and choosing to be fully present. Make time this week to watch the sun rise or set, gaze at the stars, or take a long, leisurely walk and reflect on the magnificence of God's creation. Savor God's goodness and faithfulness during this time.

2. **Remove at least three piles of clutter from your house this week.** Walk through your home and garage and identify three areas that you've been meaning to get to. Perhaps it's a closet full of clothes, a garage shelf full of projects you know you'll never get to, or a stack of papers that has collected dust. Commit to sort through these three piles. Donate extra items. Throw unnecessary items away. As you clear them out, ask God to begin working in you so that you can practice simplicity of heart.

3. **Take a hard look at your calendar.** Reflect on activities that simply clutter your life and add unnecessary stress and strain. Prayerfully consider where God is asking you to say no so that you can say yes to more of Him.

4. **Consider limiting the number of foods you eat.** With the approval of a doctor, consider limiting the variety of food you eat for one day this week. Many people around the world survive on a basic diet of rice and beans. Consider limiting for one day this week the number of foods you eat to two, three, or four foods total. As you simplify your diet for the day, prayerfully consider in what areas of your life God is calling you to practice simplicity.

Digging Deeper

Read **Philippians 4:11–13.** In what areas of life do you find yourself least content: Work? Relationships? Home? Finances? Schedule? In what ways do you find comparison to be the enemy of simplicity? How do Paul's words to the Philippians challenge you to be content no matter what the circumstance may be?

Leader's Guide

Chapter 1: The Gift of Scripture

1. Not understanding, not knowing where to begin, or not finding the time are often big struggles that followers of Jesus may face when reading and studying the Bible. Ask participants to encourage one another with ideas, solutions, or accountability throughout the week.

2. Participants may engage in this spiritual practice in different ways and times. Encourage participants to share what works for them. Consider asking follow-up questions, including: What Bible translation do you use? Do you read or study Scripture at a certain time during the day? What additional resources do you use when seeking answers to questions you have about particular passages?

3. As we read God's Word, we may find ourselves transforming from the inside out. We may find our thoughts, words, and actions toward others becoming more Christlike as we saturate ourselves in Scripture. Often, when we don't read God's Word for an extended amount of time, we may find ourselves struggling to connect with God, making unwise decisions, or having a difficult time controlling our thoughts, tongue, or actions.

4. Throughout Jesus' life and ministry, we read about Him advocating and caring for the marginalized—including the poor, the brokenhearted, the oppressed, the captives, the blind, and many more.

5. Encourage participants to share about the first time they encountered Jesus. Try to limit stories to just a couple of minutes so everyone has time to share. Set the tone by briefly sharing the first time you heard the good news of Christ.

6. **Joshua 1:8:** "This Book of the Law shall not depart from your mouth, but you shall meditate in it day and night, that you may observe to do according to all that is written in it. For then you will make your way prosperous, and then you will have good success."

   Psalm 119:9, 11: "How can a young man cleanse his way? By taking heed according to Your word. . . . Your word I have hidden in my heart, that I might not sin against You."

   Matthew 4:4: "But He answered and said, 'It is written, "Man shall not live by bread alone, but by every word that proceeds from the mouth of God."'"

   Matthew 7:24–27: "Therefore whoever hears these sayings of Mine, and does them, I will liken him to a wise man who built his house on the rock: and the rain descended, the floods came, and the winds blew and beat on that house; and it did not fall, for it was founded on the rock.

   "But everyone who hears these sayings of Mine, and does not do them, will be like a foolish man who built his house on the sand: and the rain descended, the floods came, and the winds blew and beat on that house; and it fell. And great was its fall."

   James 1:25: "But he who looks into the perfect law of liberty and continues in it, and is not a forgetful hearer but a doer of the work, this one will be blessed in what he does."

7. Often our hearts and minds are clouded by the world around us. Instead of striving to act like Christ, we end up looking so much like the world. Scripture filters and cleanses us so we may be renewed and made pure.

8. Encourage participants to combat the struggles they listed in their answer to question 1. If they struggled finding time to study Scripture, challenge them to carve out time each day to read the Bible. If they struggled understanding Scripture, encourage them to use a study Bible or get together with a friend who has been following Jesus longer and study together. If they struggled knowing where to start, encourage them to read the gospel of John or the book of Proverbs. Find out what steps each person is going to make that week and spend time in prayer asking God to speak to each participant through His Word in the upcoming week.

✤ Four Ways to Practice Scripture Reading This Week

Invite each participant to choose which exercise(s) she plans to do during the upcoming week. Make time at the start of the next gathering for everyone to share what they learned through the activity.

Digging Deeper

Answers will vary, but the Bible is meant to be a guide for discovering wisdom and hearing from God as we navigate life.

Chapter 2: The Gift of Prayer

1. Take time to celebrate the power of prayer in each other's lives as you share how prayers have been answered or hearts have been transformed through prayer.

2. Often the prayers of others transform us in a way we weren't expecting. An example may be a parent or grandparent praying for their children to come to know the Lord.

3. A life without prayer may be dull, boring, lifeless, hopeless, frustrating, or lonely.

4. Answers will vary. We often forget to pray about everyday situations as well as situations we think we can handle on our own. Prayer often reduces the amount of anxiety or worry we feel over a situation.

5. **Luke 9:18:** He prayed alone.

   Luke 9:28: Jesus prayed on the mountain with Peter, John, and James.

   Luke 11:1: He prayed in a certain place. Sometimes having a particular place in or near your home for prayer is helpful.

   John 11:41–42: Jesus prayed in front of others so that the crowd around Him would know that God sent Him.

6. Jesus came out of prayer and named the twelve disciples. Prayer shaped how Jesus responded to situations and people and can shape how we respond too.

7. Answers will vary.

8. Encourage participants to share what types of prayers have been effective for them. Others may rely on a mnemonic device such as ACTS (Adoration, Confession, Thanksgiving, Supplication) or PRAY (Praise, Repent, Ask, Yield) to help them pray. Challenge participants to branch out in their prayer life and explore a new spiritual practice when it comes to praying by picking out one of the options in question 7 or by taking a suggestion from someone else.

   As you close, spend time in prayer asking God to fill each participant with a desire and willingness to pray each day. Commit to praying for one another during the week.

✤ Four Ways to Practice Prayer This Week

Invite each participant to choose which exercise(s) she plans to do during the upcoming week. Make time at the start of the next gathering for everyone to share what they learned through the activity.

Digging Deeper

We may find times when we wrestle in prayers that others may come to know the Lord, illnesses will be healed, relationships will be mended, the wait will be over, fear will go away, or financial needs will be met. The answers we receive may not be what we expected, or we may still be waiting for a response. But as we pray—even for the toughest things—we can trust that God is transforming our hearts and minds to be more and more like Christ.

Chapter 3: The Gift of Service

1. Utilize this question as an icebreaker to get to know participants better. Spend time allowing them to share what stirs their hearts, certain organizations or ministries they admire, as well as how they are gifted to serve others—through cooking, babysitting, words of encouragement, and much more.

2. Through serving others, we learn endless lessons, including how to better understand God's heart for the marginalized, what it means to put others first, and how to love people well.

3. When we do something for others, it is hard not to want to share it with everyone around us in celebration. It also may be hard to let others take the credit for something that we did. The world tells us to shout about our successes and what makes us great, but Jesus reminds us to serve with a humble spirit.

4. **Matthew 8:1–4:** Jesus healed a man with leprosy and told him not to tell anyone.

   Matthew 14:34–36: Jesus healed many just by the touch of His garment.

   Matthew 15:32–39: Jesus had compassion and fed over four thousand people.

   Mark 10:45: Christ came to serve, not to be served.

   John 13:3–5: Jesus served by washing His disciples' feet.

5. The mother of James and John defined greatness as having the most power and being the most highly favored. However, Jesus says the greatest must be a servant—one who serves instead of one who is served. Leadership in the kingdom of God is defined as those who serve others.

6. In this passage, Jesus tells us that what we do for the least deserving, we do for Him. Often we let moments to serve others pass by unnoticed. Challenge one another to think of opportunities to serve Christ by serving others.

7. Serving with God's energy is like scooping water out of a strong waterfall—you'll never run dry. When we serve with our own energy, we are scooping from a shallow pond. Soon enough, we'll run ourselves into the ground. When we find our strength in God and allow Him to pour His love, grace, mercy, and patience into us, not only can we serve better, but we may find ourselves serving with a Christlike attitude instead of one of self-righteousness.

Spend a few minutes sharing the joys of serving others—perhaps the joy of newfound friendships, loving others by meeting needs, or showing others how loved and worthy they are.

✤ Four Ways to Practice Service This Week

Invite each participant to choose which exercise(s) she plans to do during the upcoming week. Make time at the start of the next gathering for everyone to share what they learned through the activity.

Digging Deeper

Spend time in prayer asking God how you can continue to serve others, act justly, love mercy, and walk humbly with Him in your everyday life.

Chapter 4: The Gift of Stewardship

1. Being a generous steward may be difficult for some. Remind participants that being a good steward doesn't just mean gifts of money. While being financially generous is needed, we also can be generous with our relationship, time, gifts, and more.

2. For some, it may be most difficult to be generous with their money or their time.

3. The story reveals many lessons, including the idea that stewardship is never about the amount of money you give as much as it is about the heart with which you give it. This woman's stewardship demonstrates absolute trust, wild generosity, and grand love.

4. Often we fear that what we have to give will never be enough or make any real difference. Or we may fear that we will be left with nothing if we give to others. It also can be easy to begin to judge whether others deserve what we have to give.

5. Simply meeting a friend for coffee, a small gift of time, can make a big difference in her life by encouraging her and showing her love. Perhaps you served others in a way that God used to do big things for His kingdom—such as volunteering in a children's ministry or a local soup kitchen.

6. **Psalm 37:21:** The righteous are those who give generously.

   Proverbs 3:9: We're called to honor the Lord with the best of our wealth.

   Matthew 25:14–30: We're expected and called to be good stewards of that which God has entrusted us.

   Romans 14:12: We will give an account of ourselves to God.

   2 Corinthians 9:11: We are called to be generous on every occasion, which results in thanksgiving to God.

   1 Peter 4:10: We should use whatever gift God has given us to serve others.

   Encourage participants to share with one another lessons that they have learned about stewardship. Perhaps others will glean wisdom from their responses.

7. God is the source of every blessing. While we can never outgive God, that isn't the point. Instead, we are called to be generous stewards of that which God has entrusted to us and allow Him to continue to transform our hearts into His likeness.

8. Spend time in prayer asking God to lead you to be cheerful and generous givers of all of your resources.

✤ Four Ways to Practice Stewardship This Week

Invite each participant to choose which exercise(s) she plans to do during the upcoming week. Make time at the start of the next gathering for everyone to share what they learned through the activity.

Digging Deeper

When we are generous, we are declaring that we trust God for everything in our lives. When we are stingy, we try to take control of our lives. We are acting as if we are the owners instead of God.

Chapter 5: The Gift of Journaling

1. For some, journaling may be a daily habit. Others may have started and never finished countless journals or diaries. Journaling is a great way to record God's faithfulness throughout the days, months, and years of your life.

2. Journaling isn't for everyone, and that's okay! Encourage participants to share on both sides of the spectrum, the avid journalers and the non-journalers.

3. Answers will vary. If they feel comfortable, invite participants to share a few pages of their journals as an example of how they usually keep a journal.

4. Answers will vary.

5. Answers may include descriptions such as He is faithful, loving, kind, gracious, sovereign, jealous, wise, living, active, and just.

6. Journaling and writing may not be for everyone. Encourage participants to consider what stirs their heart and mind the most—writing or speaking aloud.

7. Often we may be tempted to withhold from God such emotions as anger, jealousy, frustration, and fear. For some, journaling can be a healthy outlet for honestly expressing even the most difficult emotions to Him.

8. For some, the most difficult part of journaling is being disciplined or consistent. Encourage participants who struggle with the discipline of journaling to find an accountability partner. Others may not be able to write as quickly as they think and would prefer to simply pray without writing. Encourage participants who struggle with writing down all their thoughts to simply write one-word prayers or praises, instead of lengthy prayers.

✤ Four Ways to Practice Journaling This Week

Invite each participant to choose which exercise(s) she plans to do during the upcoming week. Make time at the start of the next gathering for everyone to share what they learned through the activity.

Digging Deeper

The psalmist in Psalm 78 records the various ways God led, directed, and saved His people over hundreds of years. Throughout all of Israel's history, God has remained faithful even when the Israelites couldn't see Him in the moment. In the same way, God is continually faithful in our lives, even if we don't always notice. Journaling is a great way to record the faithfulness of God in our lives so that when difficult situations arise, we can be reminded of God's goodness in all circumstances.

Chapter 6: The Gift of Celebration

1. David was rejoicing because the ark of the Lord was being brought into his city. He danced before the Lord in joy and celebration.

2. Michal was angered by David's rejoicing. She ridiculed him, but David responded that God had chosen him to rule over Israel, so he would celebrate!

3. Answers will vary. Reassure participants that in spite of this kind of celebration feeling uncomfortable or unfamiliar, God loves a joyful heart, and we need not be ashamed to praise Him.

4. God wants us to remember His faithfulness to us as a reminder of His unending love for His children. God loves His children so much that He provided a way out of sin and death, first through the Passover lamb, then through Jesus Christ.

5. God sent Jesus to be the Passover Lamb for all His children, a gift to spare us of the consequences of sin. Jesus was sinless and spotless, just like the Passover lamb.

6. Celebration allows us to reminisce on all the blessings we've already received, to appreciate everything we have to be thankful for now, and to look ahead in hope of what God has in store for us.

7. Zephaniah 3:17 reminds us that God rejoices over us, His beloved children. Even in the midst of our messy lives, God still loves us! How much more should we celebrate our perfect God?

8. Celebrating can be difficult for some because it may feel as if we're forgetting the issues we are facing. Rather, celebrating reminds us to focus our eyes on our Provider and Savior in gratitude for everything in our lives—the good and the bad.

✤ Four Ways to Practice Celebration This Week

Invite each participant to choose which exercise(s) she plans to do during the upcoming week. Make time at the start of the next gathering for everyone to share what they learned through the activity.

Digging Deeper

Passage	Feast/Festival	Passage	Significance in the New Testament
Leviticus 23:5	Passover	1 Corinthians 5:7	Christ is the Passover Lamb.
Leviticus 23:6–8	Feast of Unleavened Bread	1 Corinthians 5:7–8	We continue to rid our lives of the old bread, leavened with malice and wickedness, and replace it with the unleavened bread of sincerity and truth.
Leviticus 23:9–14	Feast of Firstfruits	1 Corinthians 15:20–23	Christ is raised with the firstfruits (the promise of a harvest to come).
Leviticus 23:15–22	Feast of Weeks (Pentecost)	1 Corinthians 12:13	We are baptized by the Spirit.
Leviticus 23:23–25	Feast of Trumpets	Matthew 24:30–31	Jesus will come with the sound of a trumpet.
Leviticus 23:26–32	Day of Atonement	Matthew 27:51	Jesus' death tore the veil in the temple (where the high priest offered the sacrifices).
Leviticus 23:33–43	Feast of Tabernacles (Booths)	John 7:37–38	Jesus is the Living Water.

Chapter 7: The Gift of Sabbath

1. Answers will vary.

2. Instead of spending time creating, on the seventh day, God rested. Even the God of the universe takes time to rest! In doing so, He also invites us to rest from our busyness each week.

3. The fourth commandment reminds us to keep the Sabbath holy by resting. The Israelites were called to do no work and to invite their families, servants, animals, and guests to do the same. The Sabbath extends to include even the least of these, as God invites all of His children and all of creation into Sabbath rest.

4. Those who honor the Sabbath will find joy in the Lord, triumph on the land, and feast on Jacob's inheritance, because he was the father of the Israelites who wrestled with God and prevailed and inherited the promised land.

5. Spend time having participants share what a restful Sabbath looks like for them. This could be anything from sleeping in to playing in the park to grabbing coffee with a friend.

6. Jam-packed schedules often prevent us from celebrating Sabbath. Another reason may be that we don't understand the necessity of weekly Sabbaths.

7. **Mark 3:1–6:** Jesus healed a man's hand on the Sabbath.

   John 7:23: Jesus healed a man's body on the Sabbath.

   John 9:14: Jesus healed a blind man's sight on the Sabbath.

8. Celebrating Sabbath each week may include sacrificing your to-do list and deadlines and creating a space for rest. God designed Sabbath as a way to remind His children what really matters—not the busyness of daily life, but refocusing our lives on Him.

✤ Four Ways to Practice Sabbath This Week

Invite each participant to choose which exercise(s) she plans to do during the upcoming week. Make time at the start of the next gathering for everyone to share what they learned through the activity.

Digging Deeper

God gives the gift of Sabbath as a sign of His unending love for His people. Instead of toiling away in work, observing the Sabbath reminds us that we are set apart to be God's beloved children.

Chapter 8: The Gift of Silence

1. When we make room for God to speak and we just listen, God will come near and reveal Himself in new ways.

2. Encourage participants to spend time sharing how God moved during their time of silence and solitude. Perhaps He comforted, encouraged, or challenged them.

3. Because we serve an unseen God, sitting and listening to Him can be difficult. We fill up our prayer times with our own voice and hardly leave room for Him to speak.

4. Quieting our soul challenges us to sit and be content at Jesus' feet, even if our life is in chaos.

5. Encourage participants to brainstorm on ways to counteract the distractions that pull us away from silence with God. Ideas may include having a pen and paper nearby and writing down any thought and distraction that comes up so it can be taken care of later. Some people need to find a specific place for silence, such as on a peaceful trail, away from the distractions around the house.

6. It is often difficult for us to wait on God's timing in our lives instead of taking things in our own hands.

7. Even as David waited in silence, God was still the only source of defense, rest, and salvation.

8. **Isaiah 30:15:** We will receive trust and salvation.

   Isaiah 40:30–31: Our strength will be renewed.

   When we add times of silence to our spiritual journeys, we are declaring that God is in full control of our lives. When we place our trust in Him alone, He will save, restore, and renew.

✦ Four Ways to Practice Silence This Week

Invite each participant to choose which exercise(s) she plans to do during the upcoming week. Make time at the start of the next gathering for everyone to share what they learned through the activity.

Digging Deeper

We have all prayed about something, only to hear silence in return. We may be tempted to believe that God isn't listening, but He is! He hears all our prayers. God's timing is not our own, so we must wait on Him and not lose hope. God is faithful to His promises!

Chapter 9: The Gift of Solitude

1. Our desire for solitude may arise when we are the busiest, surrounded by chaos and noise. We may find that our heart is crying out for quiet and that seeking God in the midst of noise becomes difficult and clouded.

2. Our world is in constant noise. Often people sleep with white noise in the background; quiet makes them uncomfortable.

3. God is constantly calling us to tune our hearts to Him, yet sometimes we can't hear Him or we don't listen.

4. When we don't carve out time to be with God, we can find our hearts distant from Him. Just as with a best friend, it's difficult to continue a relationship with God when you don't communicate or make an effort to give Him your time.

5. **Matthew 14:23:** Jesus went to a mountainside by Himself to pray.

   Mark 1:35: Jesus prayed in a solitary place.

   Luke 5:16: Jesus withdrew by Himself to pray.

   John 6:15: Jesus withdrew to a mountain by Himself.

   Solitude draws our hearts and minds back to God. When everything around us distracts us from what matters, solitude grounds us in who

God is and His desire for a relationship with us. When we are grounded in the knowledge of God's love, we can grow in the Spirit and bear fruit in areas of life where we are struggling.

6. God revealed Himself to Elijah in the form of a gentle blowing or gentle whisper. We can get so distracted by the noises around us that we may be missing God in the midst of it all. Practicing solitude allows us to focus our hearts on our relationship with God and produces fruit like being transformed in His likeness.

7. Solitude isn't something that happens when we're not paying attention, but rather it must be intentionally carved out. This may mean setting aside entire days of unplugging, going on a retreat, or physically leaving your house to go on a walk or run by yourself.

8. Perhaps you need to begin by practicing other disciplines by yourself, such as journaling, studying Scripture, or prayer. Be intentional about carving out time for solitude in your schedule and eventually move to incorporating silence and solitude during that time.

✤ Four Ways to Practice Solitude This Week

Invite each participant to choose which exercise(s) she plans to do during the upcoming week. Make time at the start of the next gathering for everyone to share what they learned through the activity.

Digging Deeper

Solitude offers time away from crowds and what others think of us and helps us be grounded in who we are in God's eyes.

Read the passages below and fill in the blanks with descriptions about who God says you are. How does seeing yourself as God does transform the way you think and address others?

John 1:12: I am a child of God.

John 15:15: I am a friend of God.

Romans 6:6: I am no longer a slave to sin.

Romans 8:2: I am set free.

2 Corinthians 5:17: I am a new creation.

Ephesians 1:4: I am holy and blameless.

Ephesians 1:7: I am redeemed and forgiven.

Chapter 10: The Gift of Secrecy

1. Use this question as an icebreaker to get to know each participant better. Share stories of surprise parties, secret engagements, or presents that were tricky to keep a secret.

2. Secrecy can be difficult when we are proud of our actions. We desire the approval and praise of those around us.

3. Betrayal hurts to the core, especially when we are betrayed by someone we trust. While there is always a chance to forgive, oftentimes betrayals can change relationships entirely.

4. Jesus calls us to practice secrecy in righteous acts, giving, prayer, and fasting. When we do these things in private, we are truly doing so only to honor God, not ourselves.

5.

Passage	Who Jesus Addressed	What Jesus Instructed Them Not to Tell
Mark 1:40–44	A man with leprosy	That Jesus healed him
Mark 9:2–9	Peter, James, and John	What they had seen (the transfiguration)
Luke 8:40–56	Jairus and his wife (the little girl's parents)	That their daughter was raised from the dead

Jesus knew His time had not come to be crucified and did not want to be forced onto a throne or killed before His time.

6. When we do things in secret, we do them in humility—we value God and others above ourselves.

7. Seeking approval from God has the ultimate reward, but seeking praise from others may seem instantly gratifying.

8. Consider asking a friend or mentor to hold you accountable and encourage you in the practice of secrecy.

✤ Four Ways to Practice Secrecy This Week

Invite each participant to choose which exercise(s) she plans to do during the upcoming week. Make time at the start of the next gathering for everyone to share what she learned through the activity.

Digging Deeper

Challenge participants to consider the ways they can humble themselves at home, work, and school and, in doing so, receive praise only from God, not from others. Perhaps that means buying someone's coffee without expecting a thank-you or doing a task without being asked or recognized.

Chapter 11: The Gift of Fasting

1. Use this question as an icebreaker to encourage people to get to know each other better by sharing what fasts they have done—from food to Facebook, TV to soda.

2. Remind participants that fasting is not for everyone. Special diets, eating disorders, or health issues may mean that fasting from food is impossible. Gently remind participants that fasting does not need to be from food alone! There are many other options when it comes to fasting, such as fasting from technology, unhealthy habits, and more.

3. Jesus tells us to refrain from letting others know we are fasting. He asks us to do this so we don't boast of our righteousness, as the Pharisees did.
   Jesus says that God rewards secret acts of righteousness.
   When we choose to fast, we are declaring with our lives that God is enough to sustain us, not just bread alone.

4.

Passage	Who Fasted	What Was Abstained From	Length of Fast	Result of Fast
1 Samuel 1:1–20	Hannah	Food	Unknown	Hannah got pregnant.
Esther 4:13–17; 8:4–14	All the Jews in Shushan, including Esther	Food and drink	3 days	Esther confronted the king, and he protected the Jews.
Matthew 4:1–11	Jesus	Food	40 days and nights	Jesus resisted the Devil's temptations.
Acts 9:1–18	Saul	Food and drink	3 days	Saul regained his sight and was baptized.

5. **Deuteronomy 9:18, 25:** Asking God to withhold judgment

   Ezra 8:21–23: Seeking God's protection

   Ezra 10:6: Confession and repentance on behalf of others

   2 Samuel 12:15–16, 22–23: Asking for healing

   Judges 20:26–28: Seeking God's direction

   Psalm 35:13: Humbling ourselves

   Acts 13:1–3: Commissioning people and sending them out for ministry

6. Answers will vary.

7. Isaiah 58 warns those who fast with bad intentions that their voice won't be heard. Luke 18:9–14 reminds us that those who humble themselves will be exalted and those who exalt themselves will be humbled.

   Answers will vary. Even with the best of intentions, spiritual practices can easily become more about exalting ourselves rather than humbling ourselves and being obedient to God.

8. Fasting requires discipline and prayer. When we fast from something, we must ensure that we are feasting on God's Word and ongoing conversation with Him to sustain us.

✤ Four Ways to Practice Fasting This Week

Invite each participant to choose which exercise(s) she plans to do during the upcoming week. Make time at the start of the next gathering for everyone to share what they learned through the activity.

Digging Deeper

Psalm 42 reminds us that we live not on bread and water alone but on the Bread of Life and the Living Water offered through God. When we deny our earthly desires and fast from something, we lean more heavily on God to fill and sustain us.

Chapter 12: The Gift of Simplicity

1. It is no surprise if we mark off each of the options. Life has a way of complicating itself, especially when it comes to schedules and finances.

2. Instead of focusing on who God says we are, we focus on the number in our bank account, the amount of Facebook friends we have, or how full our closets are.

3. John the Baptist (1:4–6): John lived in the wilderness, wearing camel's-hair clothing and a leather belt, and ate locusts and wild honey.

   Jesus (1:12–13): Jesus spent forty days in the wilderness with just animals and the angels.

   The disciples: (1:16–20): Jesus' disciples were simple fishermen.

4. Jesus called His disciples to practice simplicity to increase their trust and dependence on God. When we have less, we are forced to look to God as our Provider.

5. Having more often increases the stress in our lives, as there is more to take care of or provide for. Culture tries to convince us that bigger is better and more is better, but that simply isn't true. We can be content no matter what we have because God is our Provider and Provision.

6. Some may struggle giving up their time and would rather overbook and overextend themselves each week. Others may wrestle with letting go of possessions. Whether time or treasure, God calls us to let go and trust in Him.

7. When we allow room for God to provide even the simplest of things, we exhibit trust in God. We can be kept from lives marked by simplicity by wanting more, thinking our worth is measured in earthly things, and much more.

8. God may be calling you to downsize in every area of your life, or perhaps to downsize in small increments. No matter the amount, trust that God will provide as you simplify more and more of your life.

✤ Four Ways to Practice Simplicity This Week

Invite each participant to choose which exercise(s) she plans to do during the upcoming week. Make time at the start of the next gathering for everyone to share what they learned through the activity.

Digging Deeper

We may find ourselves discontented in areas of life when we compare ourselves to those around us. Sally may have better clothes. Jeff may have a nicer car. When we let go of comparison, we can learn to be content no matter what our situation looks like.

About the Author

Margaret Feinberg is a popular Bible teacher and speaker at churches and leading conferences such as Catalyst, Thrive, and Extraordinary Women. Her books and Bible studies have sold over six hundred thousand copies and received critical acclaim and extensive national media coverage from CNN, the Associated Press, *USA Today*, the *Los Angeles Times*, the *Washington Post*, and more.

She was recently named one of fifty women most shaping culture and the church today by *Christianity Today*, one of the thirty voices who will help lead the church in the next decade by *Charisma* magazine, and one of the "40 Under 40" who will shape Christian publishing by *Christian Retailing* magazine. Margaret currently lives in Morrison, Colorado, with her husband, Leif, and their superpup, Hershey.

You can learn more at www.margaretfeinberg.com. Become a fan on Facebook or follow on Twitter @mafeinberg.

Notes

Introduction

1. *Spiritual Disciplines 101: Pathway to God* (Kansas City, Mo.: Beacon Hill, 2005), 8.

2. http://www.teachthought.com/learning/how-many-hours-does-it-take-to-become-an-expert/.

Chapter 1

1. Stott, John, *The Bible: Book for Today* (Leicester: IVP, 1982).

Chapter 2

1. Brother Lawrence, *The Practice of the Presence of God*, 10th letter.

Chapter 3

1. Foster, Richard, *Celebration of Discipline* (San Francisco: Harper & Row, 1978), 113–14.

Chapter 4

1. Stanley, Andy, *Fields of Gold* (Carol Stream, Ill.: Tyndale), 2006.

Chapter 5

1. Klug, Ron, "How to Keep a Spiritual Journal," *Decision Magazine* (January 1983), 5.

Chapter 6

1. Ahlberg Calhoun, Adele, *Spiritual Disciplines Handbook: Practices That Transform Us* (Downers Grove, Ill.: InterVarsity Press, 2005), 27.

Chapter 7

1. Muller, Wayne, *Sabbath: Finding Rest, Renewal, and Delight in Our Busy Lives* (New York, New York: Bantam, 2000), 4–5.

2. Groeschel, Craig, *Altar Ego: Becoming Who God Says You Are* (Grand Rapids: Zondervan, 2013), 93–94.

Chapter 8

1. Mother Teresa, *Words to Live By* (Notre Dame: Ave Maria, 1999), 40.

2. Nouwen, Henri, *The Way of the Heart* (New York: Ballantine, 1981), 37.

Chapter 9

1. Cowman, Lettie B., *Streams in the Desert* (Grand Rapids: Zondervan, 1996), 71.

Chapter 10

1. Willard, Dallas, *The Spirit of the Disciplines* (HarperCollins: New York, 1988), 172–73.

Chapter 11

1. Allender, Dan B., *To Be Told: Know Your Story, Shape Your Future*, http://books.google.com/books?id=OHJogz05Mb0C&pg=PT290&lpg=PT290&ots=iR4i Nq2CeS&dq=fasting+and+dan+b.+allender.

Chapter 12

1. Shinabarger, Jeff, *More or Less: Choosing a Lifestyle of Excessive Generosity* (Colorado Springs: Cook, 2013), 25.

2. Stuart Sloan, Joanne and Sloan Wray, Cheryl, *A Life That Matters: Spiritual Disciplines That Change the World* (Birmingham: New Hope, 2002), 147.